belgrade theatre
coventry

Tall Phoenix

by Chris O'Connell

First performance presented on Saturday 30th October 2004 at the
Belgrade Theatre, Coventry

Coventry City Council

THIS PROJECT IS BEING
PART-FUNDED BY THE
EUROPEAN COMMUNITY

ⓑelgrade theatre
coventry

Tall Phoenix

Cast in order of appearance

Chipo Chung	Clare
John Marquez	Niall
Richard Sutton	Dale
Michael Vaughan	Trackman
Marty Cruickshank	Moira
Terence Wilton	Roy
Alicia Patrick	Doctor/Molly/Erica/Paramedic

Production

Writer	**Chris O'Connell**
Director	**Matthew Lloyd**
Designer	**Simon Daw**
Original Soundscape by	**Andy Garbi**
Lighting Designer	**Mark Doubleday**
Video Artist	**Lorna Heavey**
Carnival Choreographer	**Jill Freeman**
Production Manager	**Tony Guest**
Company Stage Manager	**Lianne Bruce**
Deputy Stage Manager	**Jane Andrews**
Assistant Stage Manager	**Beatrice Maguire**

Tall Phoenix runs at the Belgrade Theatre, Coventry, from
Saturday 30th October to Saturday 13th November 2004

Cast

Chipo Chung Clare

Chipo graduated from RADA in June 2003.
Theatre: Lynette in 'THE ANTIOCH RULES' (King's Head Season of New Writing), Dussie Mae in MA RAINEY'S BLACK BOTTOM (Liverpool Playhouse), Isabel in THE MAYOR OF ZALAMEA (Liverpool Everyman), and Ophelia in HAMLET (Nuffield Theatre).
Television: Miriam in ABSOLUTE POWER (BBC Comedy)
Film: Molly in PROOF (Miramax).

At RADA: Mary Warren in THE CRUCIBLE, Her sister in ROBERTO ZUCCO, Vittoria Corombona in THE WHITE DEVIL, Margery Pinchwife in THE COUNTRY WIFE and Antigone in ANTIGONE.

Richard Sutton Dale

Richard's theatre credits include one of the Birmingham Repertoire's transmissions festival in the Caribbean tour of ROMEO AND JULIET; Charley Wykeham in CHARLEY'S AUNT at the Stoke Repertoire Theatre; Sir Charlie Sackville in THE LIBERTINE and Antipholous of Syracuse in THE COMEDY OF ERRORS (both at the Union Theatre, London); Lysander in A MIDSUMMER'S NIGHT'S DREAM; De Flores in THE CHANGELING (Aberystwyth Arts Centre); and the title role in Jimmy Chinn's ALBERT MAKE US LAUGH.

His television roles include: EASTENDERS, HOLBY CITY, DOCTORS, COURTROOM (Channel 4), BRITAIN'S MOST WANTED, and the afternoon play series. He created the role of Robbie Wade in MAKING WAVES and played war hero Clive Tomry in BBC2's award winning DUNKIRK. He has appeared in the film TWO MEN WENT TO WAR and has also been a writer for the *Sunday Independent* in Ireland.

Terence Wilton Roy

Recent Theatre: Harry in SANCTUARY LAMP (Royal Exchange, Manchester); Prospero in THE TEMPEST (USA Tour); Regents Park Open Air 2004 Season; Sir Walter Whorehound in A CHASTE MAID IN CHEAPSIDE (Almeida); Judge Brack in HEDDA GABLER, Kent in KING LEAR; Charles in SNAKE IN FRIDGE, George in GHOST TRAIN TATTOO (Royal Exchange); Pastor Manders in GHOSTS; Uncle Silas in UNCLE SILAS (Method, Madness).

Television: THE FORSYTHE SAGA; FAMILY AFFAIRS; THE BILL; INSPECTOR ALLEYN MYSTERIES; RIDES 2; WATERFRONT BEAT; SOME DISTANT SHADOW; HENRY IV PART ONE; SOFTLY SOFTLY; DR WHO and VANITY FAIR.

Marty Cruickshank Moira

Theatre: Lady Constance in SUMMER LIGHTING, Melanie in QUARTERMAINES TERMS, Lady Rumpers in HABEAS CORPUS (Northampton); Gertrude in HAMLET, Mrs Crossbite in LOVE IN A WOOD (RSC); Mother in TWO CLOUDS OVER EDEN (Royal Exchange); Lettuce in LETTUCE AND LOVAGE (Exeter); Mrs Baines in MAJOR BARBARA (The Picadilly); Virginia in VITA AND VIRGINIA, Mrs Alving in GHOSTS, Paulina in A WINTER'S TALE (Sphynx Theatre Co.); Clare in A DELICATE BALANCE (Nottingham Playhouse); Hortense in A FLEA IN HER EAR (West Yorkshire Playhouse).
Television: MIDSOMER MURDERS (ITV) SPOOKS (BBC); DOCTORS (BBC); EASTENDERS (BBC); KAVANAGH QC (ITV); FAITH IN THE FUTURE (ITV); UNNATURAL PURSUITS (BBC).
Film: THE FOOL (Christine Edzard); ALIVE AND KICKING (Nancy Meckler).

Alicia Patrick Doctor/Molly/Erica/Paramedic

Alicia graduated from Webber Douglas in April 2004. Her roles at drama school include Didie in ALLEGRO, Jane Bennett in PRIDE AND PREJUDICE, Henriette in THE SISTERHOOD, Natasha in THREE SISTERS and Vera in THE ODD COUPLE. Alicia recently played the role of Donna Harper in DOCTORS VI (BBC). This is Alicia's professional theatre debut.

Michael Vaughan Trackman

Theatre: Ebenezer Scrooge in THE GHOSTS OF SCROOGE (Manchester Library); John Knox in MARY QUEEN OF SCOTS GOT HER HEAD CHOPPED OFF (Prime Productions); Lloyd Dallas in NOISES OFF, Charles Stanton in DANGEROUS CORNER and Noel Coward in NOEL AND GERTIE (Theatre by the Lake Keswick); Speed in 23.59 (Sheffield Crucible); Caliban in THE TEMPEST (London's Guildhall); Tiresius in Ted Hughes' adaptation of Seneca's OEDIPUS (Exeter); Jack Manninghan in GASLIGHT, Oberon and Thesius in A MIDSUMMER NIGHTS DREAM (Bolton Octagon). Other theatre productions include: THE THREEPENNY OPERA (Manchester Contact), THE MOSQUITO COAST (The David Glass Ensemble / The Young Vic), GREAT EXPECTATIONS, A CHRISTMAS CAROL, NIGHT MUST FALL, WIND IN THE WILLOWS and ALICE THROUGH THE LOOKING GLASS (Theatr Clwyd); A MONTH IN THE COUNTRY (Salisbury Playhouse), CARRINGTON (Chichester Festival Theatre), A VOYAGE IN THE DARK (The Sphinx Theatre Co/ The Young Vic), BENEFACTORS and THE WINTER'S TALE (Watermill Newbury); and AS YOU LIKE IT (Ludlow Festival).

Television includes: EASTENDERS, INVASION EARTH, PIE IN THE SKY, NO BANANAS, POIROT, THE BILL, SOLDIER SOLDIER, LONDON'S BURNING, INSPECTOR MORSE, MINDER, CRIME CASEBOOK and THE CELLULOID WORLD OF DESMOND REZILLO (in which he played 12 parts over six episodes).

John Marquez Niall

Television: PILLOW TALK (CH 4); GODS AND GODDESSES (BBC), EASTENDERS (BBC), BLACK BOOKS (Assembly), CROSSROADS (Carlton), Ray in THE BILL (Thames TV), JONATHAN CREEK (BBC), Daly in SOLDIER SOLDIER (Central), PC Bates in KILLING ME SOFTLY (BBC)
Theatre: Puck in A MIDSUMMER NIGHT'S DREAM (Chichester), I CAUGHT MY DEATH IN VENICE (Chichester), Liander in THE COFFEE SHOP (Chichester), Calchus/Menelaus in IPHIGENIA (Sheffield Crucible), Oscar in SWEET CHARITY (Sheffield Crucible), Mark in MOTHER TERESA IS DEAD (Royal Court), Lawrie in SING YER HEART OUT FOR THE LADS (National), SNOWBULL (Hampstead Theatre) FROM STREET CAR TO TENNESSEE (Young Vic), Policeman in FROM MORNING TO MIDNIGHT (ENO), Darius in LOCAL (Royal Court), Rock in BABY DOLL (Albery Theatre/RNT/Birmingham Rep), Bil in SMALL CRAFT WARNINGS (Pleasance Theatre), The Corporal in THE COLONEL BIRD (Gate), Benvolio in ROMEO AND JULIET (Greenwhich Theatre), Parkis in THE END OF THE AFFAIR (Salisbury Theatre), A MIDSUMMER NIGHT'S DREAM (Orange Tree), Konstantine in THE SEAGULL (Orange Tree), Perry in ALL MANNER OF MEANS (BAC), Billis in SOUTH PACIFIC (Drill Hall), Sam in I ONLY WANT TO BE WITH YOU (White Bear) La Mota in THE LAST DAYS OF DON JUAN, Dan in AN EVENING WITH GARY LINEKER (Birmingham Rep).

Production

Chris O'Connell Writer

After winning a Pearson Television Theatre Writers Bursary, Chris was Writer-in-Residence for Paines Plough, 1999-2000.
Work to date includes, for Theatre Absolute, CAR, RAW and KID. (CAR and RAW won Fringe First Awards for Outstanding New Work and Innovation at the Edinburgh Fringe Festivals 1999 and 2001 respectively. CAR also won a Time Out Live Award for Best New Play on the London Fringe, 1999); THYESTES, for RSC; HYMNS, for Frantic Assembly; HOLD YA', for Red Ladder Theatre Co; SOUTHWARK, for Paines Plough; COOL WATER MURDER, for Belgrade Theatre; THE BLUE ZONE, for mac Productions; GABRIEL'S ASHES and COOL WATER MURDER for BBC Radio 4. His work has been both read and produced in America, Australia, Italy, and Estonia. Chris is currently Playwright in Residence at Birmingham University attached to their M(Phil) in Playwrighting and has run writing workshops at the Actors Centre, the Arvon Foundation, Goldsmith's College, and is under commission to the Plymouth Theatre Royal.

Matthew Lloyd Director

Matthew was formerly Associate Director at Hampstead Theatre, where he directed the following new plays: the multi-award-winning THE FASTEST CLOCK IN THE UNIVERSE, LION IN THE STREETS, A GOING CONCERN, THE MAIDEN STONE, GHOST FROM A PERFECT PLACE, SLAVS!, THE ELEVENTH COMMANDMENT, APOCALYPTICA and, most recently, the Olivier Award-winning THE LUCKY ONES.
He was Joint Artistic Director of Manchester's Royal Exchange, where directing credits include: AN EXPERIENCED WOMAN GIVES ADVICE, ALL'S WELL THAT ENDS WELL, THE ILLUSION, PRESENT LAUGHTER, AN EXPERIMENT WITH AN AIR-PUMP (also London transfer), SO SPECIAL, WAITING FOR GODOT, DREAMING, THE WAY OF THE WORLD, TWO CLOUDS OVER EDEN, THE DISPUTE, THE CRITIC, A MOON FOR THE MISBEGOTTEN and THE FALL GUY.
Other credits include: DEMOCRACY (Gate Theatre); the award-winning THE PITCHFORK DISNEY (Bush Theatre); 2 SAMUEL II, ETC (Theatre Upstairs); THE L.A. PLAYS (Almeida); THE HOME SHOW PIECES and LA RONDE (Citizens' Theatre); A MIDSUMMER NIGHT'S DREAM (Leicester Haymarket); MEASURE FOR MEASURE and DEATHWATCH (Tomi Theatre, Off-Broadway); CLOUD NINE (Parco Theatre, Tokyo); THE ENGLISH AMERICAN (Soho Theatre); and most recently FLY (Liverpool Everyman). Opera includes: THE BARBER OF SEVILLE (Scottish Opera).
He is currently Artistic Director of the Actors Centre. Forthcoming work includes new plays by David Schneider and Charlotte Eilenberg, and THE ODD COUPLE (Liverpool Playhouse).

Original Soundscape by **Andy Garbi**

Andy Garbi is one of the leading torchbearers for cross-genre music whose cutting edge composition and vocal work has gained the support of leading artists in all fields including the virtuoso Kennedy and Birmingham Royal Ballet director David Bintley.

His international reputation for composition is equally matched by his performances, the most recent of which (representing the UK for music at the City of Birmingham Symphony Orchestra Centre) earned him a commendation from the Royal Netherlands Embassy and the Arts Council of England. Andy has also made headline appearances at high calibre festivals across Europe, including Glastonbury and Terschelling's 'Oerol' (Netherlands). His maverick approach of 'urban meets esoteric' strongly resonates with the plays of multiple award winning Chris O'Connell, producing scores for Theatre Absolute's Street Trilogy and nightclub based Bluezone.

He sings with legendary cult band 'suns of Arqa' and co-founded the acclaimed group 'headhunters'. His solo album is due for release in 2005. Andy has also just won the Channel 4 Film Music Award 2004. andy@garbi.fsnet.co.uk

"Extraordinary music" The Scotsman

"Virtuoso Playing" Making Music magazine

"Reminiscent of Dead Can Dance" Birmingham Post

Simon Daw Designer

Simon studied Fine Art at Glasgow School of Art followed by a Postgrad at Motley Theatre Design Course, London. He has exhibited photography, film, video and installation work in both the UK and abroad, most recently in the form of his installation/performance piece SEA HOUSE commissioned by the Aldeburgh Festival.

Theatre design credits include ROMEO AND JULIET (Royal Shakespeare Company), ADAM AND EVE (TPT, Tokyo), six plays for the IMPRINT YOUNG WRITERS FESTIVAL (Royal Court Theatre Upstairs), THE CHANGELING (NT Studio), RAFTS AND DREAMS and ACROSS OKA (Royal Exchange Studio, Manchester), RELATIVELY SPEAKING, THE WITCHES, EVERYMAN and HABEAS CORPUS (Northampton Theatres), UNDER THE CURSE and TRAGEDY: A TRAGEDY (Gate Theatre), TOUCHED (RSAMD, Glasgow), THE SINGING GROUP and EXCLUDE ME (Chelsea Theatre), FRAGILE LAND (Hampstead Theatre), THE ARBITRARY ADVENTURES OF AN ACCIDENTAL TERRORIST (NYT, Lyric Hammersmith Studio), KES (NYT, Lyric Hammersmith).

Design for film includes THE FALL (35mm, National Film and Television School).

As co-director of the arts company Scale Project, Simon has collaborated on site-specific performances in Harlow Town Hall, The Arches, Glasgow and in a Siberian nuclear bunker.

Mark Doubleday Lighting Designer

Mark Doubleday was trained at LAMDA where he won the Richard Pilbrow prize. Since then he has lit over 200 productions in most of the UK regional theatres as well as in Europe, USA, India, South East Asia and South America.

Most recent productions include: EUGENE ONEGIN, MTL; LE NOZZE DI FIGARO, Opera Zuid, Netherlands; HANSEL AND GRETEL, Scottish Opera Go Round; MANON, Die Fledermaus, English Touring Opera; THE BEGGAR'S OPERA, A CHORUS OF DISAPPROVAL, HENRY IV PARTS I & II, Bristol Old Vic; FALSTAFF, RAM; ARIADNE AUF NAXOS, Aldeburgh; LE TOREADOR, MESSALINA, AMADIGI DI GAULA and I GIARDINI DELLA STORIA, Batignano; DIE ENTFÜRUNG AUS DEM SERAIL, Läckö Slottsopera, Sweden, A NITRO AT THE OPERA, ROH2; SIX-PACK, Tête à Tête/ENO Studio and FAMILY MATTERS, a newly commissioned opera also for Tête à Tête. LA FANCIULLA DEL WEST, NORMA, Opera Holland Park; SHADOW OF A GUNMAN, Tricycle Theatre. Future Plans include: RAPE OF LUCRETIA, RCM; REVIVAL!, ROH2.

Lorna Heavey **Video Artist**

Lorna Heavey is a cross-platform artist, interested in exploring the integration of disciplines, collaboration and the search for meaning derived from unexpected combinations and visual confrontations. She studied Fine Art at Chelsea School of Art, Kingston University and Dusseldorf Academy where she specialised in performance and video installation. She has recently worked as a video artist for the theatre collaborating with Filter Theatre at the National Theatre Studio for GRYTPYPE, Rupert Goold at Theatre Royal Northampton for GRYTPYPE, Complicite for GRYTPYPE for the Royal Court, Tom Morris at BAC for GRYTPYPE, Paul King for GRYTPYPE for the This Way Up Tour. As artistic director of Headfirst Foundation, Lorna is involved in a wide range of projects involving, theatre making, film, art installation and music which has led to collaborations with numerous DJs, Design Council, RSA, ICA and RIBA.

ⓑelgrade theatre
coventry

The Belgrade Theatre was built in 1958 as part of the reconstruction of Coventry after World War II. It was named in honour of the gift of timber from the former Yugoslavia used to help reconstruct the city. Holding 866 in its two-tier main auditorium, it remains one of the largest regional producing theatres in Britain.

The theatre has a long history of producing new writing with early Company members at the Belgrade including Trevor Nunn, John Gunter, Joan Plowright, Michael Crawford, Frank Finlay and Leonard Rossiter, with Arnold Wesker and David Turner among the new dramatists. The Belgrade is also the home of the Theatre-in-Education (TIE) movement, and continues to pioneer new initiatives in this field as well as other community and outreach programmes. 2006 will see the opening of a new 250-300 seat second space and refurbishment of the existing listed building in which the theatre can expand the range of work it produces and invites to play Coventry.

Hamish Glen has led the theatre since 2003 and his artistic policy ensures a commitment to the production of more new drama, such as Tall Phoenix, in the future.

belgrade theatre
coventry

Belgrade Theatre Staff List

Board of Directors
Chair **David Burbidge OBE DL**
Vice Chair **Sue Wilson**
John Blundell
John Clarke
Carol Malcolmson
Kumar Muthalagappan
Alistair Petterson
Peter Pinnell
Martin Ritchley
David Shortland
Tony Skipper

Management
Artistic Director **Hamish Glen**
Executive Director **Joanna Reid**

Finance
Head of Finance **Andrea Simpson**
Accounts Manager **Linda Alger**
Payroll Officer/Accounts Assistant **Nicola Boyle**
Capital Project Accountant **Surjit Sandhu**

Administration
PA to the Chief Executive/Admin Manager **Denise Duncombe**
PA to Executive Director **Angela Naylor**
Admin Officers **Christine Dimond, Liz Hunter**

Events
Producer **Jane Hytch**

Community and Education Company
Associate Director – Community Company **Justine Themen**
Theatre Projects Officer **Linda Leech**
Youth Theatre Director **Jenny Evans**
Acting Out Project Manager **Jenny McDonald**
Community Company Administrator **Debbie Hewitt**

Production
Head of Production **Tony Guest**
Company Stage Managers **Lianne Bruce, Steve Cressy**
Deputy Stage Managers **Jane Andrews, Sara Austin-Wells**
Assistant Stage Managers **Beatrice Maguire, Elizah Jackson**
Production Assistant **Rita Smith**

Head of Lighting/Sound **David Muir**
Deputy Chief Electrician **Glyn Edwards**
Assistant Electrician **Caroline Shirville**
Sound Operator **Chris Mock**
Head Prop Maker **Sherri Hazzard**
Head Scenic Artist **Laura O'Connell**
Deputy Scenic Artist **Sandra Field**
Head of Wardrobe **Margaret Lock**
Deputy Head of Wardrobe **Mandy Brown**
Wardrobe Assistant **Julie Morgan**

Marketing
Director of Marketing **Antony Flint**
Press & PR Officer **Ray Clenshaw**
Marketing Officer **Jess Thomas**
Marketing Assistants **Lori Ford, Angela Tamufor, Helen Tovey**
Box Office Manager **Eamonn Finnerty**
Box Office Sales Assistants **Linda Grimmett, Valerie Gunter, Christine Jackson, Kaye Moore**
Marketing Volunteers **Helen Arnold, Maureen Connoll, Joan Howard, Doris Webb**

Front of House
Theatre Manager **Jonathan Bainbridge**
Assistant Theatre Manager **Carol Tomlinson**
Front of House Manager **Margaret Rogers**
Duty House Manager (part-time) **Sue Smith**
Senior Usher and Duty Manager **Kate Copland**
Ushers **Lee Barnes, Sarah Benn, Eddie Brewster, Jennifer Chatfield, Lori Ford, Sheila Hart, Samantha Please, Doreen Smallman, Sandra Stockwin, Colin Turner, Dan Whitfield**
Housekeeper **Christina Ivens**
Cleaners **Moira Barker, Maureen Billings, Irene Cheston, Jackie Gardner, Wayne Gardner, Maureen Hicks, Barbara Thompson**
Senior Maintenance Officer **Paul Duncombe**
Maintenance Officer **David Eales**
Access Officer **Judith Ogden**
Audio Describers **Keith Bradbury, Jess Thomas, Will Wiltshire, Phil Woodcock**
Sign Language Interpreters **Clare Edwards, Anji Gregg, Rachel Tipping**

Catering
Catering Manager **Lynne Craig**
Head Chef/Deputy Catering Manager
Gavin Stevens
Catering Supervisors **Stacey Craig,
Christopher Pearce**
Catering Staff **Selina Braithwaite,
Michael Duffy, Clement Dupreneuf,
Mairetta Gallagher, Nell Jones, Charan
Kaur, Mindy Kaur, Michelle Mooney,
Joseph Sherriff, Glenn Sherlock**

Capital Development Scheme
Project Director **David Beidas**
Project Manager **Buro Four**

Architect **Stanton Williams**
Structural Engineer **Flint and Neil**
Services Engineer **Rybka**
Theatre Consultant **Theatreplan**
Acoustics **Arup Acoustics**
Access Consultant **All Clear Designs**
Planning Supervisor **Quoin Consultancy**
Cost Consultant **Davis Langdon and
Everest**
Head of Fundraising **Jill Mowlam**

Thank you:

Bite Communications Ltd
Blue Coat School, Coventry
Sampson Lloyd Pub, Smethwick, Birmingham
Stanton Williams
St John's Ambulance, Coventry

TALL PHOENIX

First published in this play in 2004 by Oberon Books Ltd
521 Caledonian Road, London N7 9RH
Tel: 020 7607 3637 / Fax: 020 7607 3629
e-mail: oberon.books@btinternet.com
www.oberonbooks.com

A catalogue record for this book is available from the British
Library.

ISBN: 1 84002 511 5

Cover image by Oyster Design

Printed in Great Britain by Antony Rowe Ltd, Chippenham

Introduction

Tall Phoenix isn't about Coventry. It's a fictional city. In the play, Dale describes this city where he lives, and that he constantly photographs.

'...the dip, the curve, the rise and the pull. Capture the feeling. Stand and stare into the belly of the place where you live, understand it in as many ways as you can.' To some he might appear to be a fruitcake, but for me his obsession is understandable, because we can become blasé about where we live. We can stop picturing it in our mind's eye: location, land, hemisphere. Walk your city's streets and consider it; that in the scheme of things, although you know only a few people, you share the same land with thousands of others; the will, the needs, the losses and the gains of everyone are shared within the shape of things. We are individual, yet part of a community. *Tall Phoenix* is an attempt to express the endless cycle of city life, the functional, the defining, the rootless, and for me, the absolute poetic nature of cities.

Isn't it true that cities echo to the experience of generations past, and that those experiences can inform us, providing texture so that we might understand our lives now? Yet for others, the experiences of the past are an interesting irrelevance, because a city is only alive when it's in the present, or perhaps more tantalisingly, when it's imagined for the future. For the dynamic leader, for the social engineer, a city is a thing to be developed, a landscape in which to generate income, create employment, better facilities, improve the view, and leave behind a legacy.

Although cities always have, and always will continue to change, it's the nature of change and the negotiation of our common space that *Tall Phoenix* bears witness to. How, as communities, do we navigate our way though an increasingly disparate and presentational sort of world, where we are told by developers what it is that we need, and by architects how 'it' will look. Enter the character of Niall; he's traditional, scared of change. He says: 'This city was about survival. After the war..It was crushed. But "Apple Blossom Time" was playing, men and women walked around in long overcoats and smoked unfiltered cigarettes. There were trams…' He's unrealistic in his desire to keep things as they are, but has an obsessional sense of what is being lost in the name of progress. 'Yes', he says, 'the city looks better than it did twenty five years ago, you'd expect it to, but don't kill us with the rhetoric…'

With Niall, there's always the 'but'. It's where the play sits. Cities will either brutalise, or influence the well being of the people who live there. They aren't inanimate postal references, they live and breathe, and we have to be careful with them, because they are keepers of my experience, and of yours. Right now.

Chris O'Connell
Oct 2004

To the memory of
John Venn
who worked at the Belgrade Theatre.

Characters

ROY – early 60s

MOIRA – late 50s

TRACKMAN – late 50s

NIALL – mid 30s

CLARE – early 30s

DALE – mid 20s

MOLLY* – late 20s

ERICA* – late 20s

DOCTOR*

NURSE*

PARAMEDIC*

* These characters can all be played by the same actress.

A provincial city. Spring.

*The symbol / indicates an interruption point
for the following line.*

For Baggy

To Joe, Reub, mum, dad, and Helen

1

Evening.

Silence.

CLARE walks into the space.

She is in the street. She has an address on a piece of paper that she refers to. She stands and looks ahead of her, looking, watching, and sounds of the city grow.

They grow and get louder, as...

2

Evening. CLARE stands where she was, and NIALL, behind her, speaks at a meeting in a church hall.

NIALL: ....of course, that city's invisible now. It'll never feel the same as it did then, it can't. The buildings that stand around us, they were fashioned on something *he* used to stand for: grit, trust, group effort. Not the flash, not the corporate. Can someone tell me, what's so appealing about this 'corporate' lifestyle? this...I don't get it, I don't see the attraction. Why is it some people want to sacrifice, you know, *tear* down a fantastic pre-war cinema like the Gaumont in order to construct some state of the art revolving six storey laser-lit restaurant that delivers a panoramic view of the city and looks *exactly* like a bloody revolving laser-lit restaurant should look like, or to design a village of bijou townhouses (*town* houses), what does that mean?, that only a select few can afford to live in. Why do they do that...where's the *soul?* And the developers don't eat in the restaurants, the councillors don't live in the town houses, but they persuade us that these developments are what this city needs. I think you're like me, you think to yourself, 'They must be social engineers, they must have a vision, musn't they?' Or maybe they don't, maybe these days life's just ego. 'I designed that building. *I* made that happen.' Well I've got news for people like that, this isn't some fucking playground to cream a few bucks selling land and space that belong to *us*. This is a city of joy, and it's a city of pain. I never thought I could discover so much in a place so small. It's not London, it's not New York, yet it's like a million invisible cities; it's a keeper, a maze. And Roy West used to sup from the same cup. Does he think he can change this place beyond all recognition, and we won't bat an eyelid? Listen when we speak Mr West, be humble, accept our patience, be grateful for our patience.

NIALL punches his fist into the air.

No. Fucking. Spin.

3

Evening. Music plays.

DALE balances, walking to the centre of a gas pipe that spreads from one side of a stream to the other. Ahead of him is the city. He gets to the middle, sets up a shot and focuses his camera on the view of the city before him.

He presses the button and visual images of the city explode back at him, shattering across the stage.

4

Evening. The sounds of a train and the ambience of a railway station. MOIRA and TRACKMAN with bags and a suitcase.

MOIRA walks ahead. She stops, frozen, unsure. TRACKMAN catches her up.

TRACKMAN: Alright?

MOIRA: Dizzy.

TRACKMAN: That's the two hour delay.

MOIRA: It wasn't two hours.

TRACKMAN: According to my watch it was. Sit down.

MOIRA: Where?

He stands a suitcase on its end. MOIRA perches on it.

Is there any of that water left?

TRACKMAN gets some water from a shopping bag he carries.

As MOIRA drinks, he looks inside it.

TRACKMAN: Do you want these sandwiches? They're a bit warm.

MOIRA: (*Quietly.*) No.

TRACKMAN: Do you?

MOIRA: *No.*

Beat.

TRACKMAN: You alright?

MOIRA: Coming back here…

TRACKMAN: I'll help you.

MOIRA: Huh.

TRACKMAN: (*Unwrapping one of the sandwiches.*) Why wouldn't I?

MOIRA: All you've ever done is make cars. You've got big bulky fingers, your nails are split and dirty. When's the last time you did something useful?

TRACKMAN: (*Eating the sandwich.*) I'm here, aren't I?

MOIRA: I didn't mean to be fierce.

TRACKMAN looks at her. He bags the sandwich again and goes to a bin, where he dumps the shopping bag and its contents.

MOIRA: I just don't want to be your little project. Like you think you can find a reason somewhere else, use someone else to keep yourself alive.

TRACKMAN: *Is that what you think I do?*

MOIRA: Calm down.

TRACKMAN: I am calm. I'm just insulted.

MOIRA: Sorry.

MOIRA is getting money from her purse.

TRACKMAN: What're you doing?

MOIRA: I owe you a week's cash.

TRACKMAN: Not here.

MOIRA: It's yours.

TRACKMAN: So just give it me at the end of the week.

MOIRA: (*Sees how he has taken offence.*) I didn't mean…

TRACKMAN: You never do. Moira, I do a lot for you, and I don't do it because I love you, or to make you love me…

MOIRA: Well that's nonsense for a start.

TRACKMAN: Yes. But I… (*Beat.*) The cash is nice, I like to earn money. But don't serve your bloody status on me.

Silence. MOIRA 'looks' at the noise around her.

Until:

If you take a mosey round, then we'll get the next train back, alright?

MOIRA: What?

TRACKMAN: It's ridiculous. We don't even know if Roy still lives here.

MOIRA: I don't want to go back, why are you suddenly saying we should go back?

TRACKMAN: I'm not.

MOIRA: We've only just arrived. Have you got the address of the hotel?

TRACKMAN: That's about the tenth time you've asked me.

MOIRA: Can I see it?

MOIRA has her hand out. TRACKMAN sighs, digs a piece of paper out of his pocket. He hands it to her.

(*Reading it.*) Okay.

5

Evening. The meeting is ended and NIALL puts papers and petitions into his bag. CLARE approaches.

CLARE: Making your getaway?

Beat.

NIALL: My...? Hello again.

CLARE: Hello.

NIALL continues with the papers.

Not such a good speech tonight. I thought the audience were losing interest.

NIALL: Maybe I was put off.

CLARE: How much do you pay to hire the hall? Does this 'campaign' have a benefactor?

NIALL: Yeah, millions pumped in. An anonymous donor in Saudi Arabia with a passion for post-second world war architecture.

CLARE: What were you put off by?

NIALL: Seeing you again. It's unsettling, staring into the enemy's eyes.

CLARE: The enemy?

NIALL: Well, a part of the enemy; the enemy's eyes by proxy. (*Beat.*) Did he send you?

CLARE: Who?

NIALL: Councillor West.

CLARE: Why would he do that?

NIALL: Because I bother him.

CLARE: No you don't.

NIALL: Bollocks.

CLARE: Seriously.

NIALL: So why won't he talk to me until the consultation?

CLARE: Because that's what consultations are for.

Pause.

NIALL: How many meetings have you been to now?

CLARE: Tonight's my third.

NIALL: And he's not bothered?

CLARE: It was my choice, he didn't send me. (*Beat.*) I even bought a campaign badge. You should make that your official by-line. 'No Fucking Spin.' Will you put it / on for me?

NIALL: Don't mock.

CLARE: I'm not. I'll wear it for half an hour, until I meet Roy.

NIALL: You're meeting him tonight?

CLARE: Catch up session. He's been away, conferencing in Europe.

NIALL: Yeah. Five thousand pounds…how many of them? Five councillors at a cost of how much?

She offers the badge again. He takes it and they stand close.

CLARE: You're very good. When you get into your stride, you're really engaging. A campaign's only as good as its leader.

NIALL: Who are you quoting? And who's calling it a campaign anyway? I just don't want the council to knock down the bloody Gaumont. What I say makes sense. Why do you think so many people have signed the petition? It's their city, it's their vision that has to count.

The badge is done.

CLARE: I heard you're a teacher. What subject?

NIALL: History.

CLARE: I'd like to go back to school. Please sir.

NIALL: What is this?

CLARE: I just support what you're doing.

NIALL: No. You're PA to the leader of the council; it's not allowed.

CLARE: I'll be finished at eight.

NIALL: …Listen, I don't…I'm married…Will be; soon. I just want to do my thing, alright? Get West's back up, ruffle a few feathers.

He packs his bag again.

CLARE: Who is it you're marrying?

NIALL: Deborah.

CLARE: And?

NIALL: Nothing. None of your business.

CLARE: Now you're clamming up. When you're up there you're so watchable. I can't imagine you're really this tight -lipped; all that Irish flannel.

NIALL: Listen, I was born and bred here, yeah? My dad was born and bred here. I'm not even second generation. I didn't even know my old man's dad, alright? My old man doesn't even know where the fuck his dad hails from; he went to Kerry for the weekend, one of the few trails he had, stood on a green hill, drank two Guinness, didn't feel a thing, came back to England. Bang. Just…this place.

CLARE: Yes, but when I see you, when I listen to you talking, you look and you feel….Irish. Sorry.

She puts her coat on. She slides her card into his pocket; he puts his hand in, pulls the card back out. Holds it.

NIALL: Go and write up your notes for Mr West and the rest of his cronies.

CLARE: They're not cronies.

NIALL: Telling people what to think.

CLARE: That's what they're elected for. Bye Niall.

NIALL: Bejaysus, so you are, so you will, so it is, so I do…

He goes. She watches him leave.

6

Late evening. MOIRA is in her hotel room and she unpacks her suitcase. Re-folding her clothes, she looks out of the window, unsure, nervous.

Music grows, and DALE climbs to the very top of a ladder attached to the side of a high building. It's dangerous, but he presses on, determined.

TRACKMAN enters. MOIRA turns and smiles. He sits on the bed, playing with the door key of his own room. Until…

TRACKMAN: Is your room okay?

She nods.

DALE: Tall Phoenix, rose from the fire of the city that was set alight. Ten times. Ten fires. It walked through the city, it did didn't it? Above the city, the roofs and the flames. Tenth time, tired always rising.

Reaching the top, DALE focuses his camera. He takes a shot of the city. The image of the city fires back at him, splintering across the stage.

And then he falls.

MOIRA: I'm going for a walk.

7

Late evening. ROY's office in the town hall. ROY sits alone.

CLARE enters. ROY is taking various plaques out of a cardboard box, examining them dubiously.

CLARE takes off her coat, and crosses to ROY. She kisses him.

CLARE: You're sweaty.

ROY: Long day. You been home?

CLARE: Out.

ROY: I love the sound of this place when everyone's gone for the day. (*Of the plaques.*) These look a bit cheap.

CLARE: I think Newton'll tell you it's a budget thing.

ROY: I know. It's just…what's this bit?

CLARE: It's the coat of arms.

ROY: I know what it is. I mean the material.

CLARE: They're plaques. It's a bit late to change things Roy.

ROY: I'm not having a go.

CLARE: You are.

ROY: I'm not, I just…I'm the leader of the council. First impressions. (*He thumbs the plastic.*) Our first Community Awards next week, and they could break.

CLARE: They won't.

ROY: I know plastic. My idea, my community awards, but I don't get any say in the matter.

CLARE: The meeting was held over a month ago. February 23rd. You were on a trip to Berlin.

ROY: So no one faxed anything through?

CLARE sits on the edge of the desk.

CLARE: Shall we do these notes? I could be booked elsewhere.

ROY: Why'd you say it like that?

CLARE: Like what? I *am* booked elsewhere.

ROY: Is that what you think, like you've got me hooked around your little finger? (*Beat.*) You haven't.

CLARE: You can't resist me.

ROY: That's because you're sexy as fuck.

CLARE: Roy, you're sixty, you're overweight, and you smoke too much. Does that make you happy? Does your wife soothe you like I do? No.

Beat.

ROY: Okay. So you have got me wrapped round your little finger. But that's not… I'm actually happy about that.

CLARE: (*Sharp.*) So don't criticise me.

ROY: Fucking imp.

CLARE: (*Laughing.*) Imp. What kind of a word is that?

ROY: Clare, I'm not some… It's me in charge, you know?

CLARE: Out moded, / out of date.

ROY: You forget sometimes.

CLARE: Yes, but that's because I see two sides of you don't I?

ROY: Precisely. So when you're *here*, behave accordingly. Next month the PM's visiting. I can't have you being my secretary, and you're all, 'Roy this, Roy that.'

CLARE: Are you 'special' then?

ROY: I… (*He stops.*) You know what I'm saying. The New Park Project, the Community Awards, the City Carnival, the Central Aviation Initiative. The pride in this fucking city. (*He is at the window.*) That's what the PM's visit is going to mean, it's going to shatter some bloody preconceptions, wake the country up to what I've been doing here the last ten years. You could write me a description of this place…but keep the name of the city secret, list everything you can get here: the business, the shopping, the bloody…

He stops, breathing suddenly, pushing through some sort of low level panic. CLARE watches him impassively; it happens quite often.

ROY: …the businesses who've chosen to re-locate here, the clubs, the nightlife, the motorway network, the trains, right at the heart of the transport network…

CLARE: Slow down.

ROY: …can't say fairer than that. And you'd want to come and live here. Guaranteed. But then tell everyone the name of the city and you'd be like: 'Oh, is that where it is? 'Maybe not.' *Pre-conceptions.* That's what the PM's visit is going to do. Shatter a few bloody pre-conceptions about this place.

CLARE yawns.

That's rude. Did you see this yet?

Now he's on a roll, the patter is helping his recovery. He flicks off the lights.

CLARE: Roy, now's not a good time.

ROY: Not sex. Better than that.

Virtual images, designs of a city, begin to appear around them. The design is daring, bold, inspiring, all conceived through smart and expensive specifications and building materials. It keeps rolling as they talk, one street after another, inside buildings, side on, front on, rear views, cut-aways.

If we're building, then we need to feel it.

He clicks an icon and 'opens' a door into a swish looking block of flats. The images play around them and CLARE watches both the images, and the pleasure they give to ROY.

CLARE: I prefer our normal kind of foreplay.

ROY: *Entrance* halls; the scourge of modern day tower blocks. Here, they're as important as the home itself, no dark corners to rape, or sell drugs in. (*He lights a cigarette, loving the taste of it.*) Lights, sofas, parquet flooring. Fifteen, twenty years from now, you won't recognise this place.

CLARE: What a salesman.

ROY: Get on board!

CLARE: I am. I'm there. (*She goes to him.*) Although of course, I'm prepared to acknowledge more than you ever will.

ROY: About what?

CLARE: (*Of the images.*) This.

ROY is mesmerised.

The art of illusion. How about colour? There…

She points to some cobalt blue wall tiles. ROY peers at the image. Her hand goes to his cock, rubbing him.

The colour on the screen is never the exact same colour you see when it's re-produced. (*ROY breathes.*) Computers can make you believe in anything.

ROY leans into her, lets her rub. Until he pulls away…

ROY: This body won't sag.

CLARE: I won't let it.

They are laughing.

I need to do your notes.

ROY: (*Lighting another cigarette.*) Who is it you're meeting?

CLARE: Someone.

ROY: There you go again.

CLARE: Like an imp?

ROY: Am I funny?

CLARE: Roy, try not to treat everything as a threat all / the time.

ROY: How's it a threat? People love me. (*He hands a letter to her.*) 'As Prime Minister, I am delighted to offer my personal support to your city's Community Awards…'

CLARE: I saw it.

He snatches it back, sits.

Long silence. ROY watches CLARE as she sorts papers on her desk.

What?

ROY: Nothing.

She continues.

CLARE: (*Laughing.*) *What?*

ROY: (*Laughing.*) What is it? What's your agenda? You can do any job, you're over-qualified.

CLARE: Yes, but I want to be where you are now. I want to be a politician. So I need to learn the trade. Twenty years as a councillor, you've done it all. When I've achieved what I want at local level, I'll go and start shagging an MP. I'll start lesson number two.

ROY and CLARE laugh. She moves in and kisses him. It's long, they undress each other, mainly ROY's clothes coming off. She nibbles at his ear.

Don't act like you don't care about me…. Don't act like you don't… I'm a treasure, for you… I'm a treasure, to fight for… Treasure… Yours…

She pushes him back onto the desk, gets him going, and then pulls away.

I better do those notes.

ROY: What…?! Fuck's sake…Clare!!

She sits at her desk, gets some paperwork.

CLARE: This stuff, it's the ratification for the last street trading review. I'll read it to you… 'The purpose of this report is to advise the Cabinet…blah, blah, following publication of its notification to change the existing street trading controls within the city centre area.' Do you want me to go on?

She waits. ROY is still on his back on the desk, his trousers round his ankles.

ROY: I….

8

Night. Music plays.

A trolley crashes through the door into the city A&E department. DALE is on it, drifting between consciousness, bloodied from his fall. A nurse pushes the trolley, and a doctor holds an oxygen mask to DALE's face.

DOCTOR: Dale…? *Dale*…my name's Lucy… Can you hear me?

He loses his breathing and starts to gasp for air. The doctor pushes the mask back onto DALE's face and he drags the air down.

Another image of the city shatters across the hospital ward, and DALE watches its image as it passes over him, driving him crazy, still dragging the oxygen down into his lungs.

9

Music plays. NIALL breaks through the back doors of the Gaumont Cinema. He goes to a window where he ties a banner so it hangs outside. It reads :'No. Fucking. Spin.'

10

Night. CLARE stands on the roof of her flat. She wears pyjamas, smokes. With her cigarette, she lights a newspaper. It glows red, and she holds it out, dropping it over the edge. She takes a glass bottle and holds it out, drops it, unflinching at the sound of it shattering. Sitting on the edge, she pours a glass of water slowly, into the darkness.

She lies back, still smoking her cigarette, impassive to the stars, and the sound of the city moaning around her, from where, in the distance, comes the sound of a piercing scream.

11

Night. The street. TRACKMAN runs to MOIRA.

TRACKMAN: Moira!… Where the hell've you been, it's three in the bloody morning?!

MOIRA: Is it?

TRACKMAN: What're you doing? Did someone hurt you?

MOIRA: I wanted to walk.

TRACKMAN: What happened?

MOIRA: There were some lads passing, pisspots on their way home. I shouted at them.

TRACKMAN: What?

MOIRA: I shouted at them. 'Come on, you're a bunch of nancy boys… You couldn't piss your way out of a paper bag.'

TRACKMAN: Really insulting stuff then.

MOIRA: I was thinking, 'What do people say to each other these days? How can I make them really angry!' They started coming towards me.

She is laughing.

TRACKMAN: Listen…

MOIRA: I wanted them to attack me.

Pause.

TRACKMAN: Jesus.

MOIRA: If I'm really here, *now*… I don't know Track, if I'm going to see him, it's like I needed something, for remembering…

TRACKMAN: It's three o'clock. *We're in a deserted bloody street.* (*Calmer.*) We should be at home. That's us, that's what we like.

MOIRA: Not anymore.

TRACKMAN: *Just be aware that I'm clocking all of this.*
Alright? If I think you're losing it, I'm calling the whole
thing off, it's over.

*He stops, as NIALL appears. They are by the Gaumont.
Shortly due for demolition, it is fenced off with construction
hoardings. NIALL is squeezing through a gap between the
hoardings. The two parties are mutually surprised by each
other.*

NIALL: Shit… Hi…(*Beat.*) Can you help me?

No answer.

…I'm just…

*MOIRA walks to the hoarding, stares past NIALL and up at
the Gaumont, at the sheer height of it.*

TRACKMAN: (*To NIALL.*) What are you doing exactly?

NIALL: Can you just help me? (*He struggles to get free again.*)
…I can't see what I'm caught on.

*TRACKMAN reaches through and grabs NIALL's leg. He
rips the material of NIALL's jeans free.*

Cheers.

MOIRA: Do you work in there?

NIALL: Are you joking me?

MOIRA: My God, it's the Gaumont.

NIALL: (*He glances up at the cinema.*) Nearly a hundred feet
high, where'd you ever see a front like that? What the
hell made someone build that, in a place like this? It
doesn't matter, it's here, and it's magnificent. (*He points
up at the banner.*) I broke in.

MOIRA: You're a revolutionary then.

NIALL: I do my best.

TRACKMAN: Stand there much longer, and we'll be on CCTV.

They look towards a CCTV camera that has begun to change position. Their faces appear in projection as they look back towards the Gaumont.

12

Night. NIALL's house. He comes in with tea on a tray. MOIRA is at the window, TRACKMAN on the sofa. NIALL hands MOIRA a mug of tea.

MOIRA: Thanks. (*She drinks.*) Dramatic view.

NIALL: Not bad.

MOIRA: Right opposite the Gaumont. Is that why you bought it?

NIALL: Been here since my mum died.

MOIRA: Do you mind us coming back?

NIALL: You looked frozen. (*He sinks into the sofa.*) Need a good cuppa after a night like tonight.

TRACKMAN: Next time go on a diet.

NIALL: I've been through those hoardings a million times since they started.

MOIRA: Who's 'they'?

NIALL: The powers that be, council. I don't know, whoever it is sits on transport and environment sub-committees of bloody transport and environment sub-sub-committees, deciding what to waste our cash on.

TRACKMAN: Was it a good job, did you like it?

NIALL: I didn't work there. I went to see bands there, several times as a kid and things, same as thousands of other kids. The Smiths, The Clash, mid-80s, after they'd stopped showing films, before the bingo got a hold.

NIALL grabs a bunch of manilla folders, he chucks them onto the table and empties out some newspaper cuttings.

Look at that stuff, read it…Not just the Gaumont. (*He goes to the window.*) The whole swathe of that block, they want to knock it down.

TRACKMAN: Why?

NIALL: 21st Century initiatives, 'gentrification'…how come you don't know any of this?

TRACKMAN: We're just visiting.

NIALL: The New Park Project. Fuck, didn't we know already that we're living in the 21st century, or do we need bloody initiatives all the time just so we don't forget? Yeah, the city's a better place to look at than it was twenty-five years ago, you'd expect it to be, but don't kill us with the fucking rhetoric. There's a lot of things in this city that *haven't* changed… Try bringing up your kids on benefit on the Bellfield estate. Who cares about Gap and 'Sainsburys Local' setting up stores in some new shopping development when you're living out there, yeah?

TRACKMAN: (*Gesturing to the room they sit in.*) Which you don't, obviously?

NIALL looks at him.

NIALL: Let's have something stronger.

He gets a bottle of whisky, flicks on the CD player.

Do you like Bone Crusher and the Ying Yang Twins?

TRACKMAN: Don't start Moira off, she's an expert on the ying and the yang.

He chucks the CD at TRACKMAN. Pours more whisky.

NIALL: One of my pupils gave it to me, can't get my head round it. Next week I'll give her Pink Floyd – retaliation.

MOIRA: All this hankering for the status quo, it's going to make life one long struggle…

NIALL: Now they *are* a good band… There's nothing wrong with change, it's whether things change for the better. Down in one?

TRACKMAN: Actually, we should go.

NIALL: Trackman. What kind of a name's that?

TRACKMAN: A nickname.

NIALL: Love it. I think it's great. No need asking what you did for a living, yeah? Where're you both staying?

MOIRA: Do you know the Crispin Hotel?

NIALL: Fine, listed building; can't get their hands on that.

MOIRA: I think the technological age must have reached your school by now, or do you get your students to write on slate?

NIALL: I just know what he's trying to deny. He's trying to replace one set of values that're tried and tested, which re-built this city after the war, with another set that's short term, and basically not fit to piss on.

MOIRA: Who is?

NIALL: Roy West, Leader of the Council. I've held weekly meetings and I've staged a one-man protest outside the Town Hall every afternoon for the last month and a half. Me and Roy, face to face, show him who's boss, that's the deed, that's the mission.

Beat.

MOIRA: Roy West?

NIALL: Do you know him?

MOIRA: Yes.

TRACKMAN: (*To MOIRA.*) That's no surprise then.

MOIRA: What isn't?

TRACKMAN: Roy, leading the bloody council. He always said 'They can't keep a good man down.'

MOIRA: (*Irritated.*) Is that right? (*Beat.*) Niall, have you got any food? Sorry, I don't think they'll do anything this late at the hotel.

TRACKMAN: They'll be making breakfast.

MOIRA: (*To TRACKMAN.*) Do you mind...!? (*To NIALL, indicating the kitchen.*) Can I just...?

NIALL: Be my guest.

NIALL waves MOIRA through to the kitchen.

MOIRA: Get some food inside me, and I'll be all ears.

13

Night. Music plays. CLARE's roof. She walks round in circles. She has her iPod on, lost in the music. As she finishes one cigarette, she lights another from the end of the first one.

14

Night. Still in NIALL's flat. MOIRA is in the kitchen.

NIALL: (*Of the bottle of whisky.*) Are you having some?

TRACKMAN: It's nearly four in the morning.

NIALL fills TRACKMAN's glass anyway.

NIALL: What's the situation with you and Moira? Is she your wife?

TRACKMAN: No.

NIALL: So what?

TRACKMAN: She used to live here. I lived here myself. I worked at the car plant.

NIALL: What's the Roy West connection?

TRACKMAN: I can't tell you any of that.

NIALL: Why not?

TRACKMAN: I'm not going to contribute to your vendetta.

MOIRA comes back in, carrying a bowl of cereal.

MOIRA: Twenty-three years ago, me and Roy were living together. Him and Trackman were shop stewards. I worked as a librarian in town.

NIALL: And?

TRACKMAN: And nothing…

MOIRA: And me and Roy had an altercation…

TRACKMAN: (*Standing.*) It was nothing, she's…

NIALL: She's what?

TRACKMAN: Come on, we're going…

TRACKMAN takes MOIRA's arm to guide her to the door, but she shakes him off with a sudden impulse of violence that sends the cereal bowl crashing to the floor. TRACKMAN lets go and she pushes him against the wall. Long silence as NIALL watches them. Finally, TRACKMAN touches MOIRA's cheek, and she steps aside. He sits. MOIRA stays by the door.

More silence.

Until…

Sorry about your carpet.

NIALL nods.

NIALL: You found some cereal then?

MOIRA scoops up the cereal.

MOIRA: (*To NIALL.*) I want to see Roy.

NIALL: So?

MOIRA: Well where does he go, day to day?

NIALL: He's everywhere, you can't bloody miss him.

MOIRA: Do you know his movements?

NIALL: Not really. I'm not exactly on his Christmas card list. (*Beat.*) You can stay if you want. Shall I get you a quilt?

TRACKMAN gets MOIRA's coat.

TRACKMAN: Thanks. We should go. (*To MOIRA.*) You need a good night's sleep.

15

The absolute dead of night.

DALE lies in a bed on a darkened hospital ward. A low fluorescent light picks him out.

The oxygen mask is still on his face, and he breathes: in, and out. In, and out.

16

Morning. ROY is in his office. He speaks on his mobile to CLARE, who is in the street.

NIALL, wearing only a bath towel at his waist, sits in his flat at the window. He sits in a shaft of sunlight, enjoying the pleasure of the warm spring sunshine.

ROY: … Clare. Stop. Why haven't they printed *my* name? It's not difficult.

CLARE: I can ask someone.

ROY: They've mentioned the PM…

CLARE: Good.

ROY: …and they can mention Arsene Wenger too, they can mention Donald fucking Rumsfeld for all I care, as long as they put my name next to it. Don't just *ask* Clare. I want a full-blooded explanation. An autopsy.

CLARE: It's a small error.

ROY: Is it Newton's department?

CLARE: Yes.

ROY: Just get him to explain to me why I can't be included on my own press release.

CLARE: I'll make sure he sorts it.

ROY: Good. (*Beat.*) You alright then? Nice night last night, where'd you go?

CLARE: I can't remember.

ROY: I went to a Mexican. Do you know it? New place, just opened?

CLARE: Where?

ROY: Didn't look.

CLARE: Roy, you must / know…

ROY: Steen Street. Very nice.

He lights a cigarette.

Ta. Bye.

ROY hangs up. CLARE is outside NIALL's ground floor flat. She pockets her mobile, brushes her hair, and rings the doorbell. NIALL answers the door, poking round it to conceal his half nakedness.

NIALL: Oh. (*Hand to his towel.*) Ooops.

CLARE: Sorry to get you up.

NIALL: You didn't.

CLARE: Well, out of the shower.

She steps inside.

NIALL: I had half a leg out.

She is staring at him.

I'll get dressed.

CLARE: You're okay.

NIALL: Won't take a minute.

CLARE: Don't do it on my account.

Pause.

NIALL: What did you come round for?

CLARE: Isn't that obvious?

NIALL: You're an early riser.

CLARE: I bet *you* are.

NIALL: What?

CLARE: I said…

NIALL: Clare.

CLARE: You can tell me to go.

NIALL: Shouldn't you be at work?

CLARE: There's enough time to do both.

NIALL: Both what? I…

CLARE: You want me as much as I want you.

NIALL: I'm not like you think.

CLARE: Men of principle are the best.

NIALL: You've come all this way across town just to /…?

CLARE: I usually get what I want.

NIALL: Don't ruin things.

CLARE: Like what? We've only met at your 'sermons', we don't have anything to smash or lose here. I just want to fuck you.

NIALL: (*Laughing.*) Since when?

CLARE: (*Shrugging.*) Since when do you say no to something like this?

NIALL: Always.

CLARE: Everything's temporary Niall. Learn that, and we'll have a much better time.

Pause.

You're like a monk.

NIALL: I've just…I'm…

CLARE: Sure.

Beat.

NIALL: I'm speaking again tonight.

CLARE: I'll check my diary. (*He fiddles with his towel.*) That conscience…grappling.

NIALL: Not at all.

CLARE: Sure?

NIALL: Never more so. (*Beat.*) It's at the Methodist / Hall in…

CLARE: I'll see. If not, maybe another time.

She kisses his cheek, and goes.

17

Morning. In the hospital. DALE lies in bed, holding his camera, looking to the window and the city beyond.

DALE: Tall Phoenix, tired from city growing, after the fires, city loud, city too much closer. Phoenix started walking, it did didn't it? Sweeter land. Sheltered there. It did didn't it? Tall Phoenix, sat. Phoenix alone. Thought of things. How much it wanted things. Tall Phoenix, it did didn't it? Tall Phoenix, sat and thought of things.

18

Morning. ROY is in the toilets at the Town Hall, dragging down a cigarette. CLARE knocks on the toilet door, she puts her head round.

CLARE: Ready?

He turns away.

What is it?

No answer.

You need to pick yourself up.

ROY: Is the meeting set?

CLARE: Everyone's waiting.

ROY: Tell them I'm coming. Tell them it's me.

CLARE: They know. (*Pause.*) You're Roy West.

ROY: That's what I was just telling myself. Do you love me?

She kisses his cheek. He stubs out his cigarette, and they leave.

19

Afternoon. MOIRA and NIALL in a pub.

NIALL: Another?

MOIRA: I can drink five more. Just five. Then I'll stop. I usually drink six.

NIALL: You've already had three. (*Beat.*) Another anyway. Loosen the vocal chords.

MOIRA: Loosen them, go on.

NIALL: It's nice to drink with a *drinker.*

MOIRA: Let me pay.

NIALL: No. (*Beat.*) You really remind me of my mum.

MOIRA: Now that's got to be a compliment, otherwise you wouldn't dare say such a thing.

NIALL: It is. She was… You're honest. My mum was a teacher, that's why I do it. I loved the way she went off in the morning with a bag full of books, marked them by the fire in the evening, loved the way she handled me; firm, nurturing. She trained in that post war time, knew the rights and wrongs; you knew if she said something, it had to be true. Teachers don't lie do they, like, what's the gain for a teacher in lying? Politicians, money makers, there's a reason. Teachers, why would they lie about maths, about english?

MOIRA: About history?

NIALL: Even that.

MOIRA: You're filling young heads.

NIALL: Yeah. So be responsible, give them something to emulate.

MOIRA: Do you ever worry about burn-out?

NIALL: It's a quality.

MOIRA: Don't get me wrong, I'm pissed…

NIALL: Don't mock me.

MOIRA: I've noticed it before, people like you, you love the sound of your own voice, but you won't accept that one day people might not want to listen.

NIALL: What's wrong with being principled?

MOIRA: Nothing.

NIALL: What's wrong with my mum being a hero?

MOIRA: Heroine.

NIALL: Yeah. To me. She stood for fucking…

MOIRA: She stood for Fucking? Good woman.

NIALL: *Listen…*

He stops.

MOIRA: We're both a bit…What star sign are you?

NIALL: Doesn't matter. Yeah, I am a bit…

MOIRA: Fiery.

NIALL: Kids absorb the things around them. If a man stands on a podium and tells a lie, they copy it.

MOIRA: But no one did that in the past?

NIALL: They did, but more people…*believed* in things, didn't they?

MOIRA: Some of them did.

NIALL: You knew who your enemies were.

MOIRA: We thought we did. The past is what you feed on. There's nothing wrong with that.

Pause.

Did you think about what I said last night?

NIALL: You mean Roy?

MOIRA: Yes.

NIALL: Moira, you're alright, but I don't know if I can help you. I'm busy doing my own stuff with Roy. He's my sworn enemy, I'm not the one to introduce you to him,

Her mobile starts ringing .

MOIRA: Do you know where he lives?

NIALL: No.

MOIRA: Sorry… I'm still listening, can you pass me my…

NIALL: Your what?

MOIRA: My, the thingy, what's the word…too much to drink…

NIALL: Lipstick?

MOIRA: No, the…

NIALL: Cuddly toy?

MOIRA: My handbag!

They are laughing.

Give it to me.

He chucks it, she catches it and digs out her phone.

(*Mobile.*) Hi Track… Sorry, where are you? Yes, I'm alright, stop fussing for God's sake… I'm with Niall. I went to meet him at his school… We're in a pub. The…

NIALL: Pig and Drum.

MOIRA: The Pig and Drum. (*Then to NIALL.*) God, is that where we are, I used to come here, I was far too old for it, but the music was great. (*Back to TRACKMAN.*) Yes, I am. *Very* drunk. I'll get a cab… *Yes.* Bye. (*She hangs up.*) I think he actually likes it when I wander off and get a bit pissed, I'm always more relaxed like this.

NIALL: What makes him follow you round the country?

MOIRA: Two weeks after he found me wandering at Weymouth train station, the silly bugger seized up with a slipped disc. I looked after him. We've ended up together, and over the years we've tried to love each other. It's always failed; because of me, because of the way I am. He thinks it's him. And it's not. The man breaks my heart.

NIALL: But he looks after you.

MOIRA: I pay him to be my minder. If we do it formally, we know where we stand. It's not much, it's not like the minimum wage or anything like that.

NIALL laughs.

I've been getting worse.

NIALL: What do you mean?

MOIRA: Erratic.

NIALL: What's wrong with you?

MOIRA: I can't forget.

NIALL: About what?

MOIRA: But maybe that's a good thing.

NIALL: What is?

MOIRA: Not forgetting. It's better to deal with it head on. Today I feel… (*She thrusts her fist forward.*) Just believing I can do it.

NIALL: How come you were wandering at Weymouth train station?

MOIRA: Breakdown.

NIALL: What made you go to Weymouth?

No answer.

NIALL: Did you go there with Trackman?

MOIRA: No.

NIALL: Is this to do with Roy?

Beat.

MOIRA: Yes.

She looks at him. Looks away. Beat.

NIALL: I'm still none the wiser. (*NIALL lifts his glass to drink, and looks at his watch.*) Shit! (*He drinks up.*)

MOIRA: Can I come to the meeting?

NIALL: What? (*Beat.*) I don't know, suit yourself, yeah…? But I'm going to go on ahead, I need to get my speech finished… (*Leaving.*) You know where it is… Methodist Hall…

NIALL is gone. MOIRA looks into her glass.

20

Afternoon. Music plays. TRACKMAN sits contentedly on a wall, sunshine beating down on him, birdsong caught in the blare of the city noise. He tries to open some sandwiches, sealed in tight plastic packaging. Even for someone of his strength, he can't make headway, and grows increasingly frustrated, trying to get a grip with his nails, trying to pierce it with his teeth.

As he gives up with a sigh of exasperation, CLARE passes on her way back from coffee-break, sipping on a take-away Cappuccino. She hesitates mid-step for a second, as if she might help TRACKMAN. He looks at her, but then she continues, swiftly breaking their moment of contact.

TRACKMAN takes an apple from his bag, and bites into it.

21

Afternoon. DALE is in the hospital ward. Moving gingerly on his feet, he has his camera. Speaking as he works, he takes considered, careful shots of the city outside.

DALE: Tall Phoenix, comes to Babba-lacu; as far as the eye can see. Quiet, birds feeding, drinking on its edges. Sweet land lies across Babba-lacu. Phoenix waiting, wondering, it is, isn't it? 'What's life on the other side?' Tree trunks down, and Tall Phoenix, working with its beak, chopping, pecking, builds the boat, sails river, sails Babba-lacu. Find more. To live more. It does, doesn't it? Tall Phoenix, free from city, or boat turns back. Does it? Or Tall Phoenix says no, city be without me; it can be can't it?

22

Late afternoon. TRACKMAN is in an employment office. He stands before MOLLY, an employment clerk.

MOLLY: Take a seat again.

They sit, and MOLLY glances through an application form he's just filled in.

Sorry to keep you. Have you got a few minutes?

TRACKMAN: Now?

MOLLY: I need to go through a few things with you.

TRACKMAN: Okay.

MOLLY: Are there any referees you can list?

TRACKMAN: Where?

MOLLY: On your form, you haven't put any referees down. When's the last time you were in work?

TRACKMAN: 1981.

Pause.

MOLLY: Is this a serious application?

TRACKMAN: Yes.

MOLLY: I'm not being funny, but coming in here, you're…
Your age might go against you. If we're going to try and
place you with someone I think it might be difficult. (*She
looks at his form again.*) Is it really 23 years since the last
time you worked?

TRACKMAN: I was made redundant. I live in Weymouth.

MOLLY: What do you do?

TRACKMAN: Keep busy, run a boys club, boxing,
training. I'm the treasurer. I'm on a disability allowance.
But I can do some work, (*He taps the application form.*) this
kind of work I think.

Beat.

MOLLY: What made you come in today?

TRACKMAN: I saw your advertisement, it was on a
hoarding where the car plant used to stand. I've been out
and about this morning, all over the city. Everything's
like it used to be. Not totally, but…I didn't realise how
much I'd missed it. (*Beat.*) I started on the cars as an
apprentice. There was a boxing gym in the social club…
Wintergreen oil and sweat.

MOLLY: I don't know about that, where was that?

TRACKMAN: Arrowbridge Road. You've got a call centre
opening there.

MOLLY: Not us. ADSure.

TRACKMAN: Them. That was the sign I saw. ADSure.
'Wanted: operators, cold callers.' I know about that, I've
heard about it.

MOLLY: So have you worked in telesales before?

Silence.

I appreciate you coming in to see us, and I'm trying to
be honest with you… But I can't see how you can qualify

for any of our positions, you don't have any experience, you're almost 59…

TRACKMAN: Next Wednesday.

MOLLY: Is it?

She looks at the form again.

Right. And you live in Weymouth. That's the address you've put down. Do you have any relatives living up this way?

TRACKMAN: No one really. I just happened to come back here. It's a long story.

Pause.

MOLLY: Sorry.

TRACKMAN: I get it all the time. (*Beat.*) Fifty-nine.

MOLLY: How many jobs have you applied for then?

They are laughing.

TRACKMAN: Six, seven.

MOLLY: Serious?

TRACKMAN: On a weekly basis. I'm a serial job applier. Why not? I worked half my life like a dog, I can't pretend I don't ever want to work again.

MOLLY: Just enjoy your time off. I would.

She sees him out.

TRACKMAN: Nice to meet you.

MOLLY: And you.

23

Evening. NIALL addresses an audience in the church hall. CLARE watches. MOIRA, standing apart, watches also.

NIALL steps forward and throws his typewritten speech to the floor.

NIALL: … okay, listen, I'll chuck away the speech, alright? This is getting me down, you're such a dejected looking bunch, and I can't stand it! We're not beaten, *we won't lose this campaign.* Where's the vibe? (*Grabbing papers from a table.*) This fucking petition's not good enough, why haven't we got more names on it?! (*He chucks the petition in the air. Arms out.*) *Eh?* You're me, and I'm you, and we can either get on with that and make some waves, or we can just give it all up. I know what *I* want to do. You're not going to stop listening to me, are you? No. Hands up if you're a loser, do you know what I'm saying…?! I don't think we're losers in this city. The other day I met this lad. He's 16 and he doesn't know anything about the bombs that came down on his street during the Blitz… Jesus! We had a laugh actually, he's a good lad, but I was pissed off as well because I think it's really important to know about the history of the place where you live. Don't you? And so this lad, he frowns like this when I tell him about the death toll. Yeah, *death* toll… People died for this city that night, yeah? That's why *people* should come *first,* not the sound of silence while we all…hey! (*To an inattentive campaign member.*) *Hey*…while we all sit back and take it… 'Yes sir, you're right sir, I bow to your superiority sir…' *What fucking superiority?!!* The council is elected to serve *us.* A city's not a city unless you've got *people* to fill it with for God's sake! Artifice does not *make* a city. Yeah? Has anyone got the message? People, people…everything, *anything* that's done here in the name of progress has got to be about people. Shit…you're applauding… (*He laughs.*) Cheers! (*Beat.*) Come to the consultation, we all need to be there, yeah? (*Softer.*) Mr West, I've said it to you before; listen when we speak, be humble, accept our patience, be *grateful* for our patience. No. Fucking. Spin.

The sound of applause.

24

Night. DALE, out of hospital and dressed again, is on the streets. He is in a bad way, but he throws himself to the floor, resting his camera on his bag and sizing up a shot.

In NIALL's flat. NIALL stands facing CLARE. He hesitates. She walks over to him, and they kiss.

On the road, images hurtle towards DALE, shattering across the stage; images bigger than him as he lies flat against the ground, faces and buildings passing him, trucks and cars hurtling, the city moving forward to take him in.

25

Night. At NIALL's house. He and CLARE have just made love, and they lie silently on the floor.

Long silence. Until…

NIALL: Where did you crawl from?

CLARE: A hole.

NIALL: Where all the beautiful mice live.

She kisses him.

Where do you live?

CLARE: Southside.

NIALL: Big house? Bookcases, wooden floorboards and a coffee grinder in the kitchen.

CLARE: It's in the utility room.

NIALL: Oooh.

CLARE: Are you stereotyping me?

NIALL: What do you spend your money on?

CLARE: Nothing. I save it.

NIALL: For what?

CLARE: It's impossible to do a character analysis. I don't analyse.

NIALL goes to his computer.

NIALL: Let me see. Google search. Clare... What's your last name?

CLARE: Average.

NIALL: Is there another one of you, do you think?

He taps in her name. She leans over him.

(*Typing.*) Clare...Average.

CLARE: That's where you write all your speeches.

NIALL: I download them. inspriationalspeeches.co.uk

CLARE: Can a person get a coffee round here?

NIALL: Coming up.

He goes into the kitchen, returns with the kettle lead between his fingers.

I forgot. Fuse went. Last night.

CLARE: Juice?

He goes out. She waits as the tap runs. NIALL returns with some orange juice in a kid's plastic cup.

Please.

NIALL: For my nephew. He likes to have his unkyniall cup.

CLARE has the drink in one long gulp. NIALL waits, watching her Adam's apple as she drinks.

Until...

CLARE: Aaaah.

She hands him the cup.

NIALL: You're a big kid.

NIALL takes the cup back out to the kitchen.

(*Calling from off.*) Do your folks live here? Are you from the city?

CLARE: Of course I am. But no, my parents…

She stops. NIALL comes back in from the kitchen.

NIALL: They're dead?

CLARE: Or alive. I'm not sure. My mum came over from the West Indies. I don't know which island. And then again I was born here, so why should I care?

NIALL: You have to care about things like that.

CLARE: No I don't. Not if I end up hating her for all the shit I went through.

NIALL: I'll listen.

CLARE: To what? I just told you.

NIALL: Can you trace her?

CLARE: Probably.

Silence. NIALL lies down where they started. He sighs.

And now the guilt.

NIALL: No, not guilt. I couldn't stop thinking about you. Trying to work.

CLARE: For how long?

NIALL: Months. Before you gave me your card… It's a small place… I saw you in Cobwebs, I've seen you in that Lunch Bite place. I've seen you when I've been out with Deborah.

CLARE: You're a man of real will-power then.

NIALL: It doesn't change what goes on in my head. What I believe today, I'll believe tomorrow.

CLARE: There's more to life than believing in things.

NIALL: Yeah. There's the next battle.

CLARE: Evangelism's a real turn off.

NIALL: Sorry.

CLARE: I was talking about you and Deborah.

She starts to dress.

NIALL: Why did you do this anyway?

CLARE: Do what?

NIALL: 'This.'

CLARE: I didn't do anything.

NIALL: Yeah. You came round here the other morning. And tonight you came onto / me in the pub.

CLARE: That was just to rescue you from that woman.

NIALL: Moira. She's okay. She's my drinking buddy.

CLARE: Sorry I barged in.

NIALL: I wanted you, that's the worst part. I didn't think I would.

CLARE: See.

NIALL: What?

CLARE: That certainty you swear by. Nothing's permanent. Didn't I tell you?

NIALL: So it was like a trick?

CLARE: A test.

NIALL: Fucking me to prove a point.

CLARE: Fucking you because Roy told me to.

Pause.

NIALL: Roy?

CLARE: Yeah. He said 'That Niall, he's fickle. Prove it'.

NIALL is dumbfounded.

Your *face*!

NIALL: So did he?

CLARE: What do you think?

NIALL: I…

CLARE: Of course he didn't.

NIALL: Stop messing.

CLARE: It's a joke. I fucked you because I was horny, because I knew I *could*.

NIALL: Jesus Clare…. I'm not a…some *test case*. You came onto me because you…what?… Why did you say that?

CLARE: Because I'm an imp.

NIALL: What?

She smiles at him, sweeps his hair back.

CLARE: I could get to like you lots.

Silence.

NIALL: I love Deborah.

CLARE: So are you reacting this way because I've hurt your pride?

NIALL: No.

CLARE: Is it because I'm smarter than you?

NIALL: You're smarter than everyone. You probably *have* cooked this thing up yourself. Go on, run and tell Roy…I bet you're a right fucking schemer when it comes to climbing that ladder.

She doesn't answer him.

Don't you care what I think of you?

Silence.

CLARE: My bag.

NIALL: This is crap.

CLARE: I've upset you.

NIALL: Just a bit, yeah.

She waits. She gets her bag, and goes, closing the door after her.

Outside, CLARE sits on the kerb, and adjusts her shoe. As she sits, an insect crawls past her. She watches it and lets it run onto her finger. She lifts it up, looks at it, puts it down again, and goes.

26

Night. DALE and ERICA, a CPN, in a police station interview room. ERICA enters.

ERICA: Dale.

DALE sits up.

Take it slowly. Dale, my name's Erica, the custody sergeant outside asked me to have a chat with you.

DALE: I never did anything.

ERICA: No one's saying you did. The sergeant was a little worried. When you were found, you were lying in the middle of the Eastern by-pass.

ERICA and he share a smile.

I'm a CPN, a community psychiatric nurse. I'm attached to a hospital and it's my job to be available in the community.

DALE: For loonies. (*Beat.*) I was taking a photograph.

ERICA: (*Checking her notes.*) Yes, I was reading about that. You were admitted to The General after a fall. This evening you discharged yourself.

DALE: Yes. The General by the way, is that the hospital you're attached to?

ERICA: Yes.

DALE: But on the psychiatric wing, right?

ERICA: Have you attended the psychiatric unit?

DALE: Not yet.

ERICA: Does that mean you might want to talk to someone there?

DALE: No, s'just you've got that hungry look, like you think you've scored. I'm not mad. It's cool.

ERICA: What are the photos for?

DALE: My work. I'm a photographer.

Silence.

The Eastern by-pass.

ERICA: Would you agree it's a bit unusual to lie down in three lanes of traffic in order to take a photograph?

DALE: It sounds crazy.

ERICA: A bit. (*They smile.*) Well, if you put that next to the building you climbed *and* fell from, then you're going to alert people Dale.

DALE: If the work demands, then you do it. No mad man here. I recite the story of Tall Phoenix; it's my story.

ERICA: Which is?

DALE: I went away, and I came back. Nowhere feels as fine as the place where you're born. I got a vision…

ERICA writes in her notes.

(*Edgier.*) Hey, oi…don't just write that bit down. VISION, lovely word… (*Pretending to write notes.*) 'This guy's crazy.' (*Quick.*) I got a vision. I got an equation. Coming back. I don't fit. But I know that I must. So, to capture it. Is that mad?

ERICA: Have you taken many photographs?

DALE: Six thousand and thirty-three.

ERICA writes this down. He takes her pen, holds it, stares at it as he talks.

From the perimeter. On each of the hills, looking down, (*Edgier.*) *six thousand and thirty three.* Fuck. Scope, range, the dip, the curve, the rise and the pull. Capture the feeling. Stand and stare into the belly of the place where you live, understand it in as many ways as you can. Which direction do you drive to work?

ERICA: Are you okay Dale?

He stares at her, gives her the pen back.

I come in off the motorway.

DALE: And so down the city's major artery into the centre. I know it. So how many *visions* do you have?

ERICA: Of?

DALE: Here. (*Pointing outside.*) There. Get as many angles as you can. Cover the story, and then you can write it.

ERICA: What story? Who said that?

DALE: Ernest Hemingway.

ERICA writes this down.

Or no one. The first rule of journalism.

Silence.

Erica? (*Beat.*) Can you stress to whoever reads your report, that I'm no longer disenfranchised. Alright? I'm enthused by the place in which I live. That's not a crime. That's not madness.

ERICA: No.

DALE: It's dedication. It's…

ERICA: What is it you hope to photograph most?

DALE: There's a space they could create. If only they thought about it. They're the shots I go for.

ERICA writes this down.

ERICA: Can I give you something to take for now? I'll do you a prescription. (*She writes out a prescription.*) And I'd like to make you an out-patients appointment at The General.

DALE: No need.

ERICA: Just so we can chat again. It's alright. I'll give you my mobile number. If you need me.

DALE: Let's see what you've written?

She shows him the prescription. He tries to read it, screws it up, and throws it past her shoulder.

Doctor's writing, ennit?

27

Morning. ROY's office. CLARE stands with a compact mirror. She applies lipstick. ROY sits in his chair at his desk, smoking, watching her.

CLARE: It's been getting worse.

Pause.

I mean the frequency.

ROY watches her.

ROY: Are you worried?

CLARE: Well, I might see a doctor.

ROY pours himself a coffee.

I don't sleep at nights. See my eyes now. There's bags, and there's lines.

ROY: Stress. Coffee?

CLARE: Why would I be I stressed? You're easy to work for, I don't really work for a living. I'm not a bus driver, I'm not a waitress.

ROY: You're always saying your feet ache.

CLARE: They do. (*Pause. More lipstick.*) I've been standing outside.

ROY: Where.

CLARE: On the roof of my flat.

ROY: Isn't that dangerous?

CLARE: And listening.

ROY: To what?

CLARE: Noise.

ROY: In the middle of the night?

CLARE: Yes.

ROY: (*Remembering.*) You can't sleep.

CLARE: I drop things into the garden. In the darkness, I pretend; what if there's someone, something down there that I care about? In the end I go back to bed and I lie there, listening to the clock.

ROY is breathing again, as before. He pushes through. CLARE doesn't even look at him.

I finally fall asleep, and in the morning it's like it didn't happen.

ROY: Clare.

CLARE: Am I natural?

ROY: You can't be anything with a life like that.

CLARE: I'm beginning to see that. That's why it's getting harder to sleep.

She goes to him. He holds her.

ROY: How can you be a politician?… You bang on about it.

CLARE: I know I do.

ROY: I'm training you.

CLARE: Roy the Mentor.

ROY: You're good.

CLARE: Am I?

ROY: Intelligent. Confident. So wake up. You can't 'work for the people' without having the remotest concern for your fellow citizens.

CLARE: You're not concerned for anyone.

ROY looks at her.

I mean, you don't really care for the people, or this city.

ROY: That's harsh.

CLARE: Don't you just use it?

ROY: No. This city's everything. It's here, on this land: the sun and the gold I've always been seeking… Yeah? And the people want me to find it…

CLARE: How do you know?

ROY: It's what I believe…It's for me, and it's for them. Looking for it, every little step it's like we're re-born… I wish there'd been someone like me when I was…1981, 1982…

CLARE: Why?

ROY: To use me; we needed someone to use us then… It's like you take somebody else's air, to start breathing your own. I might've died.

CLARE: (*Smirks.*) No.

ROY: Don't laugh. (*Beat.*) Who's that idiot keeps protesting outside the Town Hall?

CLARE: You know his name, don't be so nonchalant.

ROY: (*Checking the paperwork.*) Niall Devlin. That's what *he* wants to dismiss. Why should I let him do that?

CLARE: You shouldn't.

Beat.

ROY: That's the first time anyone's said that to me.

CLARE: The council backs you to the hilt Roy.

ROY: A singular voice, I mean. One that doesn't have something at stake.

CLARE: I've got plenty at stake.

ROY: True. You're loyal.

CLARE: It's not that simple. Loyalty's not the reason I stand by you. (*Beat.*) Like last night…

She stops.

ROY: Go on.

CLARE: It doesn't matter.

He kisses her. She holds onto him.

(*Quietly.*) I fucked that Niall. But I didn't do it for the city's / New Park Project, or for…

ROY: What do you mean?

CLARE: Last night.

ROY: You screwed him?

CLARE: Yes.

ROY: Why?

CLARE: (*Shrugging.*) So you can walk all over him.

ROY: You just said you / didn't do it for…

CLARE: And because… (*She stops.*) I can't articulate it.

ROY: Well I think it's clear enough… I mean, great, you fuck some guy and it's what…it's just tactics, is it? (*They face each other.*) Did you use a bloody condom…who else do you sleep with when I'm not looking?

CLARE: Roy.

ROY: You seedy little…/

CLARE: *No.* Listen. (*Beat.*) Yes, it *was* like a…tactical thing. (*Childish suddenly.*) Part of my plan.

ROY: (*Caustic.*) You've got a plan?

CLARE: Roy…

ROY: I do all the planning around here, or hadn't you noticed? What's that Niall achieved?

CLARE: In what way?

ROY: In his fucking *life.*

CLARE: I don't sleep with someone because of what they've achieved.

ROY opens his hands; like 'What about me?' CLARE goes to him.

No. You're…I don't what that… (*She tugs at his jacket.*) I want *you*. And I want you to want me.

ROY: Who said I didn't?

CLARE: Sometimes I'm scared you don't, that's why I…/

ROY: Come off it, Clare. You don't give a fuck about anyone or anything, that's the whole deal with you isn't it? You don't even give a fuck about yourself.

CLARE: I…

She stops, stares at him. Holding his look, her eyes water and she turns away, taking up her lipstick and mirror again.

You're right.

28

Morning. NIALL's house. TRACKMAN and MOIRA are at the door. MOIRA pushes past NIALL. He is edgy. As the scene plays, he polishes the house.

NIALL: … listen guys, now's not a good time, yeah?

MOIRA: You said you'd help me with Roy.

NIALL: No I didn't.

MOIRA: I just… I've been trying to work it out, if I go to that consultation, he's going to be there isn't he?

NIALL: It's his gig, yeah? / Look…

MOIRA: Right, so if I…I mean afterwards, I wanted to check with you: where will he go, will he disappear? Where I'll be sitting, will I get to see him afterwards…?

NIALL: How do I know?! Moira, I really…Things've been happening, yeah?

TRACKMAN: Listen for a bit.

MOIRA: I watched you at your meeting, you've got all the moves. So now do something for me.

NIALL: I told you.

MOIRA: When is the consultation?

NIALL: Tonight.

MOIRA: Perfect.

NIALL: No it's not, *it's not perfect because I'm not fucking ready!*

TRACKMAN: What's happened?

NIALL: You don't need to know.

MOIRA sends a table lamp flying across the room.

MOIRA: *Listen to me.*

Silence.

NIALL: I think if you're going to do that, then you should definitely leave.

TRACKMAN: She won't, she's sorry.

MOIRA: Track, I know you think you're in charge of our 'situation' up here. But you're not. So don't make a fool of yourself.

Pause.

TRACKMAN: Moira's got some problems.

MOIRA: (*To TRACKMAN.*) *Stop smothering me!!*

NIALL: Yeah, well she's like one in three, she's like one in five of us / do you know what I'm saying?

MOIRA: (*To NIALL.*) You're letting me down.

NIALL: How? (*NIALL starts polishing again.*) Like I said, this isn't me. I'm sorry. I just…I need to show people, *her*, the whole fucking lot. I can't let myself down, that's why I don't need *you* now, hassling me…

TRACKMAN: You mean Moira?

NIALL: *Her*. Clare. (*To MOIRA.*) She was at the meeting last night.

MOIRA: So?

NIALL: It's not anything that's happened to me before. She… I slept with her…I…

MOIRA: (*To NIALL.*) I've been relying on you.

NIALL: Yeah, well never rely on anyone. / It's the golden rule.

MOIRA: (*To TRACKMAN.*) Don't let him ignore me like this.

NIALL chucks the polish cloth down. Silence.

NIALL: (*Quietly.*) Fuck's sake.

Silence.

(*To MOIRA.*) Do you want a ciggie?

TRACKMAN: She doesn't smoke.

NIALL lights his own. TRACKMAN hovers, and NIALL gives him one instead.

Ta. Shouldn't really.

They smoke, and the atmosphere settles.

Ring this woman…what's her name…?

NIALL: Clare.

TRACKMAN: Ring her, and say you love her, say what you need to say to keep her.

NIALL: It's the opposite. I wish I'd never set eyes on her.

TRACKMAN: Okay. But do you agree Moira's upset?

NIALL: Seems that way, yeah. (*To MOIRA.*) What is all this with Roy, what's the big deal?

MOIRA: He ruined my life.

TRACKMAN: Moira claims he assaulted her.

NIALL: As in?

TRACKMAN: Fists. Just… (*Shaking his head.*) It's nasty.

NIALL: Meaning you don't believe her?

MOIRA: He won't agree Roy would do such a thing.

NIALL: Why?

TRACKMAN: (*Quickly, standing.*) This is / all…

NIALL: (*To TRACKMAN.*) Well I hardly know Moira, but she seems pretty fired up by something.

TRACKMAN: You're right, you don't know her. (*To MOIRA. Quickly.*) One day you're going to turn over in bed and all this need you feel for revenge, one day it's going to be gone… *Alright?* …we won't have to endure things like this…/

MOIRA: You mean *you* won't.

TRACKMAN: …we'll look back on something like this and we'll…/

MOIRA: So what 'til then?

TRACKMAN: What do you mean until then?

MOIRA: *Until then.*

TRACKMAN: Brave it out.

MOIRA: …spend the day sitting on my hands, running past the cutlery draw with my eyes closed, staring out at the sea? (*To NIALL.*) Some people like Track feel better about their lives by convincing the rest of us that there's people in this world who don't suffer.

TRACKMAN: No I don't.

MOIRA: (*To TRACKMAN.*) You keep me down there, on a cliff, and you expect me to act like I never got to suffer.

TRACKMAN: I don't 'keep' anything. You're the one moved south. What did you move south for?

MOIRA: I was confused.

TRACKMAN: You've been free to come back anytime.

MOIRA: I'm back now aren't I?

TRACKMAN: I mean permanently.

MOIRA: No Track. I'm back, and I've summoned up the courage to face him.

TRACKMAN: In order to do what? Push him under a bus? Ruin your life so he wins twice over.

MOIRA: So you agree something happened?

TRACKMAN: I'm being hypothetical.

MOIRA: Stop patronising me. (*Beat.*) Why are you so reluctant to meet Roy?

TRACKMAN: *How bloody daft is that, I'm here aren't I?!*

MOIRA: Yeah, so / you've said.

TRACKMAN: Your welfare is all I'm concerned about.

MOIRA: Well why does it feel this is about what *you* want… You can't control me.

TRACKMAN: There's a million things I can't do Moira, everyday I'm reminded of it. But one thing I can do, that

I've always done, is to try and protect you…*to get bloody Roy out of your head, to*….

He stops. They are locked into each other. Until…

MOIRA: (*Quietly.*) That's what I'm trying to do now.

TRACKMAN breaks away.

TRACKMAN: Forget it.

He goes to the door, and steps outside. As MOIRA and NIALL talk, TRACKMAN soaks up the noise of the city, lost in some kind of reverie. MOIRA watches him through the window. Silence, until…

NIALL: What sort of revenge?

MOIRA: What?

NIALL: Trackman used the word revenge.

MOIRA: I don't know what it is… (*Pause.*)… I started seeing a counsellor… (*Beat.*) I'm not a basket case. Track mocks it, but it's helped me, I don't know, it's… How long does it take before you know you're ready to face your attacker? Ten, twenty years? I just know I'm here; one day the shadows even out, you sense what it is you need.

NIALL: Why did Roy assault you?

MOIRA: Only he can he tell you that. 1981. Ten thousand men, washed up. The lot of them, laid off. Roy fought the bosses for weeks, he'd fought them all through the 70's…a right swashbuckler. He promised the union he'd save their jobs. And he failed.

TRACKMAN comes back in.

Standing in a line, his male fucking pride washed down the toilet, pissed against the wall, beer and fags like there's no tomorrow, acres of empty factories left to decay. Track was there when they put the padlocks on the gates, weren't you Track?

TRACKMAN nods.

TRACKMAN: (*To NIALL.*) Can I have another cigarette?

NIALL chucks them to him.

MOIRA: Rain and *shit* on the pavements, graffiti, dustbin bags. Track and Roy walked home together. He wouldn't let Track go back to an empty house, so he took him for a drink. (*To TRACKMAN.*) You made a toast to each other.

TRACKMAN: We made a promise. (*Beat.*) I was grateful to him for his company.

NIALL: What did you promise?

TRACKMAN: To stand by each other; that we'd rise up again.

MOIRA: Yeah, because that was Roy, taking it on the chin. How many times did he take you out drinking?

TRACKMAN: Most nights.

MOIRA: Showing off.

TRACKMAN: He was good to be with. Are you going all the way through this, by the way? (*To NIALL.*) Has she told you about Roy buying her a fridge yet...?

MOIRA: (*To NIALL.*) Ignore him.

NIALL: What's the fridge got to do with anything?

TRACKMAN: (*To NIALL.*) *You* tell me.

MOIRA: Two days after the closures he bought me a new fridge, and a new cooker; Roy pulled me along, strutting like a bloody peacock. It was like he was still shop steward, slapping people on the back, visiting the wives, their kids, keeping their chins up.

NIALL: What was wrong with that?

MOIRA: (*To NIALL.*) Because Track's got this selective memory; like we all carried on with our lives as if nothing had happened.

TRACKMAN: We did. I got up one day, and I drove for the coast.

MOIRA: *Yes… (To NIALL.) And so we're back to where we always end up. (To TRACKMAN.) How can you be so certain Roy didn't attack me?*…underneath all that buying fridges and slapping people on the back rubbish, I could see Roy crumbling…you weren't *there* Track… (*To NIALL.*) I told Roy he could cry, it was alright to feel angry…but by then the bravado thing had got ridiculous, he was slagging everyone off, all the so called 'comrades', saying *he* was the only one who could survive it all.

TRACKMAN: (*To NIALL.*) This is where I usually walk out and let her calm down.

NIALL: (*To TRACKMAN.*) Don't make fun of her. She's your best friend, and you're like… You're calling her a liar. How long can you keep calling her a liar?

Silence. TRACKMAN is contrite. He waits.

So Roy lost it?

MOIRA: Amongst other things. He said Track was a coward, that by running ran away he'd betrayed people. The city had to show it wasn't defeated.

TRACKMAN: It wasn't that easy…

MOIRA: I know it wasn't. (*Beat.*) We argued about it for days. If *you'd* gone, then things must be bad. I said it was because you were hurting, and so I used it; I told Roy it was alright for him to hurt too… 'You know Track, he doesn't walk away from anything…'

Beat.

TRACKMAN: (*This is the first time he's heard this.*) Is that what you said?

Pause.

MOIRA: One day it was late…about three in the morning, he'd been drinking, raging at how weak you were…I said it again… 'Track doesn't walk away Roy…' And then BAM! Something caved in and it all came pouring out… Why did I say it, if I hadn't said it maybe he'd have gone to bed and slept it off… 'Track doesn't walk away from anything.' I stood up for you, and he shouted, and he *roared* and suddenly he was beating the shit out of me, in the kitchen, up the stairs, beating me, my nose, once, twice, three, four, five times…because I was trying to love him…or did he hit me because he hated what he'd become…?…or because you turned your back on him…?

TRACKMAN: I… (*He stops. Silence.*) What they did to us was violent…it made us all feel… Afterwards, I was waiting for Roy to crack, and he never did. I thought, if Roy holds it together, then I can… It was hard, I'd wake up sweating… Aggression needs to be controlled, I understood that, learnt it in the gym. But what I felt when they… Violence is ugly. I did run away… I ran away from myself… (*Beat.*) If I'd stayed, I would've done the same as Roy.

Beat.

MOIRA: But you didn't stay. You're not *like* him. That's what you learnt.

TRACKMAN kisses MOIRA's cheek.

TRACKMAN: I'm sorry.

Silence.

29

Late afternoon. Music plays. High on a building site scaffold, DALE views the city.

DALE: Phoenix comes home, tall, tired. Phoenix pines city… It does, doesn't it? But city moves. Phoenix is still. City's become this, and Phoenix is still that. It does, doesn't it? Phoenix asks city to explain, Phoenix says city, *explain.* Is it, does it?

30

Late afternoon. CLARE stands outside the Council House. She smokes a cigarette. NIALL approaches with a bunch of flowers.

NIALL: Carnations. Always guaranteed to raise the pulse of red blooded romantics. Thank you for a crushing night of sex, and entrapment. I learnt a lot.

CLARE: Bollocks.

NIALL: Totally. Do you think I'd waste my money otherwise? But great, you got your kicks, well done. You've only made me more determined.

CLARE: Roy's bored by this whole thing.

NIALL: Really?

CLARE: Just leave things be.

NIALL: What's wrong with leadership?

CLARE: Is that how you see it? I don't. But that's the pleasure; your city, my city, it's anyone's city.

NIALL: What did I ever do to you?

CLARE: I hate naivety.

She stubs out her cigarette.

NIALL: You're actually quite nasty.

Silence.

Take the flowers. I quite enjoyed our...liaison. I get the feeling it was more like a maths exam for you, but that's fine, because I wouldn't want to fuck a robot twice, once is en...

CLARE hits him across the face. NIALL drops the flowers on the floor in front of her, and goes into the Town Hall.

31

Late afternoon. Music plays. Still up on the scaffold, DALE is now shooting photographs of the city. He takes them swiftly: click, wind on, click, wind on, obsessive, rhythmic.

Growing increasingly edgy, he pursues more and more shots and seems to fail with every attempt. Each phrase is accompanied by a click, and a wind on.

DALE: ...can't talk...shot of my life...Phoenix tries....come on, let's have it...shot of my life...shot of my life...shot... there...Raa! Phoenix is...shot of my life and my life's...I'm...it's there...

As he continues, he rips the negative film from the camera and starts to cut at it with a knife, re-assembling the shreds into a collage; fragmented images of the cityscape begin to fire back at him, exploding in blasts of white light.

...got it...has Phoenix got it? yeah? got it...? Tall Phoenix makes his plan, cos Phoenix *is* the city, is it does it? Phoenix destroys... Phoenix builds... Phoenix make the city... (*To the skyline.*) Let me in... you are fuck. *You are FUCKED...*

The cut-up images are coming faster at him, the white light increasing in ferocity.

Phoenix, fire.

He drops through the scaffold, not falling, but dropping, from bar to bar, until he has lowered himself to the earth.

He sits, breathing, closing his eyes.

He roars.

32

Late afternoon. The consultation in the Town Hall. NIALL, MOIRA and Trackman watch on from different areas of the council chambers. CLARE sits at the back. ROY is in full swing…

ROY: …as I've outlined before, and I want to stress this, because it's the only reason I'm here tonight, my mind was never more made up: The New Park Project is an ambitious but *progessive* plan; it'll regenerate the run down areas around the Gaumont Cinema and the central bus depot, and create a sight to behold.

NIALL: Excuse / me…

ROY: Architects, Robson and Spiller are committed to working absolutely in conjunction with ourselves…/

NIALL: Mr West.

ROY: …and with the various public art consultants concerned, so that cost, targets, and quality, which I acknowledge people have expresed concern about, are all recognised as a first priority.

NIALL: No spin, yeah?

Beat.

ROY: Sorry? (*Seeing NIALL.*) Yes, thank you Mr…?

NIALL: Niall Devlin. 'Save the Gaumont Campaign.'

ROY: Yes. And, well…all change is difficult Mr Devlin.

NIALL: I know. Just no spin, yeah?

ROY: You interrupted me, I'm entitled to reply.

NIALL: I know, just, no spin, that's all, yeah?

Beat.

ROY: I wouldn't dream of it.

NIALL: Good. While we've stopped, can I ask, is this the public bit now, is this where we get to chip in?

ROY: I hadn't actually finished.

NIALL: I know, but I hear you giving us all that, right? And I'm thinking, all you really want to do is make us look like a million other cities.

ROY: No.

NIALL: Yeah.

ROY: If you'd let / me finish…

NIALL: This city's unique, yeah?

ROY: Definitely.

NIALL: And it's unique because of the spirit that re-built it after the war, that kept it going *during* the war – neighbourhoods, pubs, shops, people taking in other people who needed help…

ROY: Niall…

NIALL: I'm still talking…/

ROY: Sorry, but there's communities like that…Mr Devlin, there's communities like that now.

NIALL: You don't go to the places I've seen then.

ROY: Yes. There's areas that are fantastic places to live, some of the most underfunded areas of the city…

NIALL: This city was about survival. After the war…

ROY: Can I conclude?

NIALL: It was crushed. But 'Apple Blossom Time' was playing, men and women walked around in long overcoats and smoked unfiltered cigarettes. There were trams...

ROY: What is this?

NIALL: It's what we had.

ROY: It's nostalgia.

NIALL: But it's what we had. I'm not ashamed to talk about it.

ROY: You're sentimental son. There's some people who are glad those days are behind us, we've come a long way since that misty eyed nostalgic crap. Modern housing, clean water, advances in medicine, the welfare state...

NIALL: Oh yeah, those old chesnuts. This is the modern world, this is progress so shut up, be quiet, watch gratefully while we waste our millions waging war, and drag our heels over third world debt because we *really* need to get our money back don't we?...

ROY: Niall...

NIALL: ...or watch while people die from famine, HIV, TB, and the pharmaceuticals play God with drugs, raise law suits to protect their patents...and yeah...

ROY: (*To those assembled.*) He's good isn't he?

NIALL: ...*watch* as we crawl closer, like, it's barely sixty years on and the NHS has become some endangered species, the hunters *desperate* to privatise it so they can run their grubby hands all over it. Yeah? This is the modern world Roy!......and we're all asking ourselves, what's gone wrong, what's.../...

ROY: We had two World Wars inside thirty-one years...

NIALL: Yeah…but it's…ask anyone if they don't worry they're being conned these days, the big 'presentation'. Ask them if they think the values we have now are…/

ROY: The bombing that you talk of so fondly…

NIALL: I don't talk about / it fondly.

ROY: Yes you do. Like it was a…I don't know, (*Scornful.*) a rites of passage, or something…The Blitz was a tragic night in which hundreds of people died.

NIALL: I'm a history teacher.

ROY: Good. So you'll know that before that, I mean, you know, 'spin', this word you've got hold of, it's not new…This thing you bang on about every day outside the Town Hall, 'No More Spin'…

NIALL: It's actually, No Fuc…/

ROY: I know what it actually is, thanks. 1937, 1938, they were 'spinning' even then. Before the bombing, there were plans on the table. Plans to pull down the city centre as it was, and re-shape it. For some people, the bombing came at the right time. Even then, things in the city were poised to change, and some people were uneasy about that. Nothing's different. So get on with it. Live with us, or leave.

NIALL: See.

ROY: What?

NIALL: Leave. Because I won't shut up.

ROY: No, leave because you'll moan about anything we try to do. Some people here, amongst it all, they forget. (*Back to the consultation.*) Now…/

NIALL: No one forgets what happened here.

ROY: You know what I meant.

NIALL: I don't. You're a poor politician Roy, you don't communicate the thought.

ROY: Did you interrupt me just so you can start insulting me? (*Beat.*) Niall, son: I've wanted to say this for sometime; I've followed your campaign with interest and you're a determined character, but then you were the same when the Ambulance service went on strike several years back, and you acted with as much fortitude when the Fire Service were on strike the November before last...

NIALL: Have you got files on people Roy?

ROY: ...and when the Stop The War coalition marched against Iraq. You're always one of the first to get in there Niall. But, and here's the point...

NIALL: I'm glad you've got one.

ROY: There's no logical argument to what you're saying.

NIALL: At all?

ROY: Particularly with this present 'campaign' you're running. Intellectually, it's shallow. I see people like you...

NIALL: People like me? What am I? Black, Asian, Irish? I'm different to you obviously.

ROY: You're what I call a headbanger...

NIALL: Don't patronise.../

ROY: I'm not, I'm just...I met dozens of people like you, day in, day out, coming to the office on the shop floor; do you know what I hated most, it was that whining sort of discontent, headless chickens, never able to be concise about what it was they were fighting for, and they were lazy because they knew someone like me was going to step in and construct the argument, focus their anger. I don't know what it is you're *angry* about, but cities do that, they deflect anger as the whiners look for someone / to blame for…

NIALL: Yeah, I *am* angry. I don't like show-offs Roy. Correct me if I'm wrong, I never did town planning at school, but if you're going to build something…a shop, a school, a theatre, it gets built because it has a function. Yeah? Why always the *grand* gesture, the sweep of the arm…Every time you and your pals sanction some elaborate new development, I get sick at the thought of someone, somewhere making money out it all!…I don't know, perhaps it's me, but it's like we're nurturing an inferiority complex here….

ROY: Not me.

NIALL: Sorry?

ROY: The opposite. No one can ever accuse me of that. I'm a proud man. I've proved that over the years; integrity, guts.

NIALL: (*Laughing.*) Is that right?.

ROY: You've had your ten minutes, time's up.

NIALL: Jesus, the arrogance of this guy.

ROY: I think we should close this consultation, sorry folks, it's been hijacked I'm afraid, and move onto something far more interesting. We've got our Community Awards coming next ladies and gentlemen, and for those of you who want to stay, you're welcome, after which be sure to come and join us outside for the passing of the city's re-vamped and newly invigorated carnival and street theatre parade, with this year's event being drawn from myths and legends of the old town.

NIALL: Roy…

ROY: We've finished.

NIALL: Not yet. I can't let that go, sorry, but that arrogance deserves…"Integrity"? You're joking me…

NIALL looks to the public gallery

NIALL: I can't see…sorry, is she there…? There's a lady in the gallery, I think she's there, she better be, she made enough fuss about seeing you. Her name's Moira. She says she knew you about twenty odd years ago…

ROY: What's this got to do with anything?

NIALL: …she might be a stalker for all I know, but she said she knew you when you were in the factories, says you weren't a very nice man, and then you got worse because you / felt so…

ROY: Because I what?

NIALL: Is this the same Roy West who beat you up Moira?

Silence. ROY looks to the gallery where he sees MOIRA for the first time. They hold a look. Until…

ROY: I don't think this is getting us anywhere.

He starts to pack up his papers.

NIALL: Roy, just so the public can get a feel for your bullshit, and your hypocrisy, Moira says you beat her up. I don't know…did you?…maybe it doesn't count anymore, because….

ROY goes.

NIALL: Don't walk away. *Roy!*

ROY is gone.

NIALL: That means I've won then, yeah? (*Beat.*) Have I won everyone?

33

Late afternoon. In the street. DALE has two petrol cans from a petrol garage forecourt. He holds them in his hands, raised cross like at waist height. He lowers them up and down, up

*and down, up and down, up and down, feeling the weight of
them, taking in air.*

34

*Late afternoon. In ROY's animation room within the town
hall. CLARE and ROY.*

ROY: *What the fuck was all that about…!!*

CLARE: I don't know.

ROY: *Who does he think he is?!!* …Why did we agree to let
him in?

CLARE: It was organised.

ROY: Bloody *dis*organised you mean.

CLARE: No.

ROY: Yes.

CLARE: You're wrong.

ROY: Right, I'm *right*.

CLARE: Are you blaming me?

ROY: *Yes…*

CLARE: Well don't.

ROY: I'll do what I want. Do you want me to / sack you?

CLARE: Do whatever you want.

ROY: Clare, I know it was *organised*, but if we're going to do
stuff like this, then we need to be sure. *What the fuck was
he up to?!*

CLARE: He's a loose cannon.

ROY: You're the one that slept with him.

CLARE: That's got nothing to do with it.

ROY: He was taking a pop at me.

CLARE: You were staging a public consultation.

ROY: Did you tell him all that stuff?

CLARE: Which?

ROY: *About Moira!?*

CLARE: Roy, you've always refused to discuss your past.

Beat.

ROY: Yeah. (*Pause. Calmer.*) Clare, I can't have you associating with people who are trying to humiliate me. How much damage is something like this going to cause?

CLARE: None, because the public will think he's an idiot.

ROY: People know he's not an idiot. Look at the support he's got.

Silence. ROY breathes, pushes through.

CLARE: What do you want to do about that woman?

Beat.

ROY: Her.

CLARE: Yes.

NIALL enters.

ROY: (*To NIALL.*) *YOU can get the fuck out!!!!!*

NIALL: Clare…

ROY: (*To NIALL.*) *Get the fuck out of my fucking office! I'll call security.*

CLARE: (*To NIALL.*) Not now.

ROY: (*To NIALL.*) You'd better come up with some sort of apology for that fiasco out there.

NIALL: It's only what Moira's / told me…

ROY: *Don't mention her fucking name.*

CLARE: (*Trying to give ROY some pills.*) Sit down.

NIALL: Is he ill?

ROY: I don't need anything, I've never felt…*I'm fucking sailing here!*

CLARE: (*To NIALL.*) *How low was that?*

NIALL: (*To CLARE.*) I warned you.

ROY: (*To CLARE.*) You knew?

CLARE: Not about that, no. He just…

ROY: *He just fucking what?*

CLARE: (*Retaining her calm exterior.*) Will you control your language? (*Beat. Of NIALL.*) He said he was angry at you. I don't know why. Perhaps you should work it out between the two of you.

She heads for the door.

ROY: (*Grabbing her.*) *Clare!*

As they struggle, MOIRA opens the door. She stops in the doorway. TRACKMAN waits behind her.

CLARE: (*To ROY; quietly.*) Let go.

ROY looks down at his hands, grasped at CLARE's arm. He looks back to MOIRA. Stepping aside, ROY sits, placing his head in his hands.

35

Late afternoon. In the street, DALE has the petrol cans. He starts to undress, until by the end he is naked.

DALE: Tall Phoenix, back, Tall Phoenix, starts the fire, new fire, it does doesn't it?… Fire again, city down, city rise…new space… And Tall Phoenix, hero, on its toes, tippy toes…. taller, bigger…

He sets fire to the clothes.

…up Tall Phoenix, city can watch you, is it, does it…?…*up! up…*

36

Late afternoon. In ROY's animation room. All present as before. NIALL sits smoking in the corner. ROY looks up. He stands and faces TRACKMAN, lost in their history, like he might offer his hand. He doesn't, he turns slowly to face MOIRA.

ROY: (*To MOIRA.*) Should I check you for weapons?

Silence.

MOIRA: (*To TRACKMAN, of ROY.*) He's sweating.

ROY: It's been a mad afternoon.

MOIRA: (*To ROY.*) No, I've seen you sweat like this before.

Silence.

ROY: Shall we get on?

ROY goes to a switch, the lights go out, and projections start to spill across the walls.

CLARE: Roy.

ROY: It's fine. She wants her pound of flesh obviously.

TRACKMAN: What is all this?

ROY: It's our animation room.

TRACKMAN: I don't mean that.

ROY: The Prime Minister's coming up next month. I'll be showing him round.

Virtual images appear, similar to those seen earlier in the play. The images keep rolling as they talk, one street after another, inside buildings, side on, front on, rear views, cutaways.

(*To MOIRA.*) What is it you want? You know that shit's in the past. Who we were, and who we are now, they're so far apart it's not worth discussing.

MOIRA: I'm the same person you left bleeding on the kitchen floor. Didn't you ever stop to think what happened to me?

ROY: I asked around. I heard you were moving away.

More images have appeared around them. Now they are strolling down a virtual street, a boulevard of open air cafes and fountains in which there are trees and wide smiling faces of people passing. ROY types over the images: THE CITY WILL INFLUENCE THE WELL BEING OF THE PEOPLE THAT LIVE IN IT.

It's printed on our headed paper. It's the credo we live by. If I could've got up each day….1981, 1982, looked at somewhere like this, then I'd've known someone cared.

MOIRA: You're kidding yourself.

ROY: Life was ugly.

MOIRA: And I told you. What did I tell you?

ROY: Are we doing this in public? Track, Clare…you can / all go now…

MOIRA: I said it was alright to cry.

ROY: (*Suddenly.*) I know what you said.

MOIRA: (*Of the images.*) This utopia won't *save* anyone. It's who we allow ourselves to become Roy.

NIALL: (*To ROY.*) What did you actually do to her?

ROY: None of your business.

TRACKMAN: Moira's travelled all the way up here, you
need to be accountable.

ROY: Don't tell me what to do.

TRACKMAN: You're a disgrace.

ROY: (*To MOIRA, avoiding TRACKMAN's challenge.*)
Compensation maybe? That's easy. But don't ask me to
beg for forgiveness, I don't need to be forgiven because I
don't have any guilt.

TRACKMAN: (*Angry.*) She's half dead, even now.

MOIRA: I can walk and talk.

ROY: That's my point.

TRACKMAN: *But it happened.*

ROY: In another place.

TRACKMAN: *Here.*

ROY shakes his head, looks at the virtual images around them.

ROY: No. You need to open your eyes Track. Some of us
have got on with our lives. Some of us stayed mate,
fought for the future. You look like you could do with a
loan, how do you get by these days?

*TRACKMAN suddenly seizes ROY by the wrist, he twists his
hand and ROY is forced to his knees. TRACKMAN is angry,
but can find no words. He releases ROY, goes to the door, and
leaves. ROY kneels where he is, shaking for a moment. MOIRA
stands above him, her fingers flexing, the violence we saw
earlier, close to the surface.*

MOIRA: All the years I've thought what I'd do to you. And
you're the same, you haven't changed. Let me in Roy.

*ROY stares at MOIRA. He gets up and turns on the lights;
the virtual images fade away. He takes out his cheque book.*

ROY: How much to cover it? My own money, not the council's.

MOIRA stares at him, she goes. CLARE is in the doorway. MOIRA stops in the doorway, looks from CLARE to ROY. She leaves.

(*To CLARE.*) How's you?

NIALL steps out of the corner he has been occupying.

NIALL: Like a bad penny.

ROY: You're certainly that.

NIALL: You're harder to crack than I thought.

ROY: Ten out of ten for trying.

NIALL: Who says I'm finished?

37

Late afternoon. Outside the town hall.

DALE is naked, he has the knife and the petrol and he is soaking it on the streets and against the sides of buidings. Close by are TRACKMAN and MOIRA.

DALE: Tall Phoenix… Phoenix, yeah?

DALE pours the petrol on himself. TRACKMAN crosses.

TRACKMAN: Hey…! Jesus…(*To MOIRA.*) Call the police… (*Going to DALE.*) Put it down son…

DALE: (*Of the city.*) You're fucked.

MOIRA: *Track…careful…*

TRACKMAN: It's petrol…!

MOIRA: *Track!!!*

He grabs DALE by the wrist, twisting him down to his knees. DALE drops the can and turns on TRACKMAN with the knife. CLARE and ROY come out to see TRACKMAN, held by DALE. DALE is naked and has a knife pointed at TRACKMAN.

DALE: Let's have it…

TRACKMAN: Roy…

MOIRA: Someone stop him…

ROY goes to DALE, he grabs him by the throat. The power of ROY's grip brings DALE to his knees, the knife falling to the floor. ROY keeps his grip, and DALE gasps for air.

Let him go now.

ROY retains his grip. NIALL comes out of the Town Hall.

Roy!

ROY: *Where's the knife?*

TRACKMAN: He dropped it, *let him go*…you'll strangle him.

NIALL: What's happening?

ROY: Fucking nutter…

Still holding DALE, ROY looks to MOIRA, to CLARE, to the others around him. They wait, as the life starts to drain from DALE. Finally, ROY lets DALE go, and DALE drops to his knees. NIALL goes to DALE.

NIALL: …alright mate…?

DALE sweeps forward and takes the knife again. He lunges towards the approaching NIALL, and sticks the knife into his chest. NIALL collapses to the floor.

TRACKMAN dives on DALE as he wheels away again, wielding the knife. He pulls him down, holding his face to the concrete.

TRACKMAN: Ring the police.

Impulsively, CLARE goes to NIALL's side; she stands above him, frozen by the expectation to act.

DALE: (*On the ground.*) Let's have it.

ROY gets his mobile out, battling to control his panic, breathing through it.

NIALL: (*To anyone, of DALE.*) …what's his…what's…?

CLARE: Ssssh.

ROY: (*Mobile.*) Yeah, police…

MOIRA: (*To NIALL.*) It's okay…

TRACKMAN keeps hold of DALE. CLARE kneels at NIALL's side. She slowly lowers her head into her hands, and tears start to pour out of her.

ROY: (*Mobile.*) An assault. It's a knife attack…the man's naked, he's… I don't know. We're outside the Town Hall. Okay… Alright…

DALE: …is it, does it?…

NIALL: (*To CLARE.*) …hurts…

CLARE takes NIALL's hand, holding it for all she's worth, until she can sustain it no longer and moves right away, watching him from the other side of the street where slowly, as the scene concludes, she re-gathers her composure.

TRACKMAN: (*To ROY; of the police.*) How long?

TRACKMAN still holds DALE. ROY takes off his jacket and covers DALE's nakedness. He looks at NIALL.

MOIRA: Is he alright?

ROY: Ambulance and police are on their way…it's alright, everyone just…

ROY keeps breathing. There are now the sounds of sirens approaching, mingling against the music of the myths and legends carnival which has started to approach.

94

TRACKMAN looks to ROY; he adjusts his hold so that ROY can hold DALE, and let TRACKMAN get up.

TRACKMAN goes to MOIRA, his arm at her waist. She turns and goes. TRACKMAN follows her.

DALE: …let's have it…

Now the carnival approaches, music blaring, and as it passes, MOIRA and TRACKMAN stop, far up the street, to see it.

CLARE stands to watch it. It is spectacular and colourful.

ROY breathes. He's okay again, he's sailing.

TRACKMAN and MOIRA drift back down, drawn towards the carnival's splendour.

A paramedic threads through the carnival. As she starts to attend to DALE and NIALL, CLARE turns to face NIALL, her back straighter now.

And then her view is broken as NIALL and DALE are obscured from view by the growing festival of the carnival.

When the carnival moves further across, NIALL and DALE and the paramedic are gone.

The last trail of the carnival passes over, and ROY walks with it, looking back at CLARE. He is past the breathing now, walking with a stride.

She looks at him, thin, soft.

He goes, his head down, avoiding the look of MOIRA and TRACKMAN, who themselves turn away, and leave.

And finally, the carnival is gone, its music distant.

The space is empty and CLARE stands alone, listening, waiting, looking out towards the city, its sounds and passions settling around her.